Encounters in the New World

A History in Documents

9

Encounters in
the New World
A History in Documents

Jill Lepore

Oxford University Press
New York • Oxford

To my nieces and nephews—Rachel and Portia;
John and Matt; Jamie, Jenna, and Kyle;
Nicholas and Carly

OXFORD
UNIVERSITY PRESS

Oxford New York

Auckland Bangkok Buenos Aires Cape Town Chennai
Dar es Salaam Delhi Hong Kong Istanbul Karachi Kolkata
Kuala Lumpur Madrid Melbourne Mexico City Mumbai Nairobi
São Paulo Shanghai Singapore Taipei Tokyo Toronto

and an associated company in Berlin

Published by Oxford University Press, Inc.,
198 Madison Avenue, New York, New York 10016
www.oup.com

Library of Congress Cataloging-in-Publication Data
Lepore, Jill
Encounters in the New World: a history in documents/
by Jill Lepore.
p. cm. — (Pages from history)
Includes index.
1. Indians—History—Sources—Juvenile literature. 2. Indians—First contact with Europeans—Juvenile Literature. 3. Indians—History—Sources.
4. Indians—First encounters with Europeans—Sources.
I. Title. II. Series.
E59.F53E53   1999
970.00479—dc21

ISBN 0-19-515491-6

Design: Sandy Kaufman
Layout: Loraine Machlin
Cover: Lenny Levitsky

1 3 5 7 9 8 6 4 2

Printed in the United States of America
on acid-free paper

Cover: *François-Joseph Bressani's 1657 map of New France.*

Frontispiece: *Théodore de Bry's engraving of Columbus's arrival in the New World.*

Title page: *An engraving of the settlement of New Amsterdam (later New York City) around 1626, when the Dutch West India Company bought Manhattan Island from the Native Americans. The settlers' cabins, a windmill, and their fort appear in this view from across the Hudson River.*

Contents

What Is a Document?

To the historian, a document is, quite simply, any sort of historical evidence. It is a primary source, the raw material of history. A document may be more than the expected government paperwork, such as a treaty or passport. It is also a letter, diary, will, grocery list, newspaper article, recipe, memoir, oral history, school yearbook, map, chart, architectural plan, poster, musical score, play script, novel, political cartoon, painting, photograph—even an object.

Using primary sources allows us not just to read *about* history, but to read history itself. It allows us to immerse ourselves in the look and feel of an era gone by, to understand its people and their language, whether verbal or visual. And it allows us to take an active, hands-on role in (re)constructing history.

Using primary sources requires us to use our powers of detection to ferret out the relevant facts and to draw conclusions from them; just as Agatha Christie uses the scores in a bridge game to determine the identity of a murderer, the historian uses facts from a variety of sources—some, perhaps, seemingly inconsequential—to build a historical case.

The poet W. H. Auden wrote that history was the study of questions. Primary sources force us to ask questions—and then, by answering them, to construct a narrative or an argument that makes sense to us. Moreover, as we draw on the many sources from "the dust-bin of history," we can endow that narrative with character, personality, and texture—all the elements that make history so endlessly intriguing.

Cartoon
This political cartoon addresses the issue of church and state. It illustrates the Supreme Court's role in balancing the demands of the First Amendment of the Constitution and the desires of the religious population.

Illustration
Illustrations from children's books, such as this alphabet from the New England Primer, tell us how children were educated, and also what the religious and moral values of the time were.

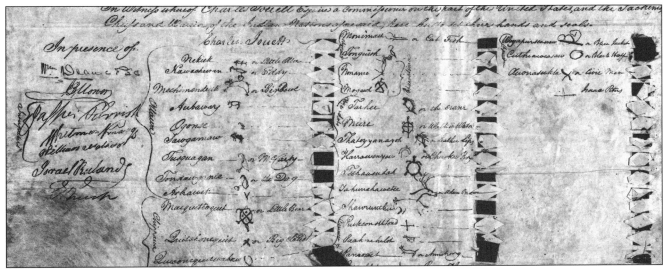

Map

A 1788 British map of India shows the region prior to British colonization, an indication of the kingdoms and provinces whose ethnic divisions would resurface later in India's history.

Treaty

A government document such as this 1805 treaty can reveal not only the details of government policy, but information about the people who signed it. Here, the Indians' names were written in English transliteration by U.S. officials; the Indians added pictographs to the right of their names.

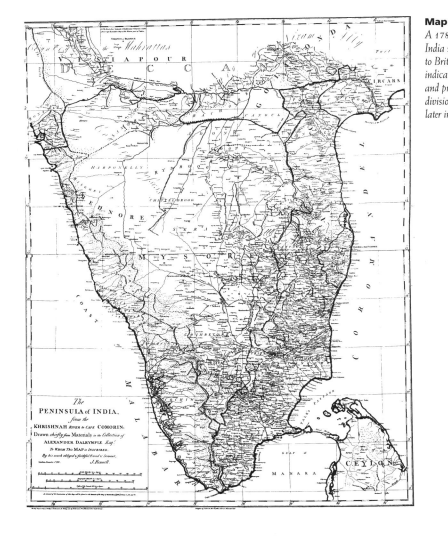

Literature

The first written version of the Old English epic Beowulf, from the late 10th century, is physical evidence of the transition from oral to written history. Charred by fire, it is also a physical record of the wear and tear of history.

How to Read a Document

This book is a collection of documents, or primary sources, from the age of encounters. Most of the primary sources in this book are written documents, often letters written by people far from home describing what they have seen and done in the New World.

Reading these documents can be a bit tricky. To understand a written document it is important to know who wrote it and for whom, when, and why. Here is an example:

Our Lord pleasing, at the time of my departure I will take six of them from here to Your Highnesses in order that they may learn to speak.

If you were to read this sentence out of the blue it would not tell you much. But if you discovered that it was written by Christopher Columbus in his ship's log on October 12, 1492, you would know a great deal: Columbus is planning to take six Indians back to Spain and present them to the patrons of his voyage, King Ferdinand and Queen Isabella.

Even knowing the circumstances in which a document is written, however, is not enough to understand it. It is important to ask more questions. Why does Columbus think his patrons will want six Indians? Why must the Indians learn to speak? Do they not speak already? It is also important to "get outside" the document and ask questions about what it does not say. What do the Indians think of Columbus? Would they want to go to Spain?

Reading documents is all about asking questions. It is not always possible to find the answers, but sometimes the questions you ask are just as important.

Cartouche

Maps usually include cartouches, or labels, like this coat of arms. Cartouches are often engravings depicting important people—monarchs, mapmakers, explorers—and provide clues about who drew the map and for whom. This cartouche is Sir Walter Raliegh's coat of arms, indicating that he governs the Virginia Colony.

Compass

This map includes a compass, or wind rose. It helps orient the viewer to north, south, east, and west. It is also a decorative element, and further enhances the beauty of the map.

Decorations

Sea creatures, whales, dolphins, fish, and sailing ships decorate the ocean on this map. A map is a document that is also a piece of art, like a painting, and mapmakers were considered artists. Just because parts of a map are decorative, however, does not mean that they should not be "read." The mapmaker drew sea creatures on this map not only to fill in the empty space but also to show sailors the ocean's dangers and wonders. Some maps from this period include half-sunken ships near coastlines that are particularly difficult to navigate.

Spelling

Spelling was not standardized until the 19th century, and books printed before then often spell words differently than we do today. For example, some people spelled "war" w-a-r, others w-a-r-r, and others w-a-r-r-e. None of these spellings were considered wrong.

Title and Sub-Title

Old books usually have long titles that are in fact whole sentences describing the contents of the book. Today, books usually have a brief description of the contents on the back, or on the jacket flaps, but centuries ago readers read the title and knew what the book was about.

Printer and Location

This book, like books today, has an "imprint"—a line indicating where, when, and by whom the book was published. The imprint can tell you a lot about the contents of a book. This book about a war between the Indians and the British colonists was printed in Boston, the capital of the Massacheusetts Colony, the year the war was won. Is it likely to mourn the Indians' loss or celebrate the colonists' victory?

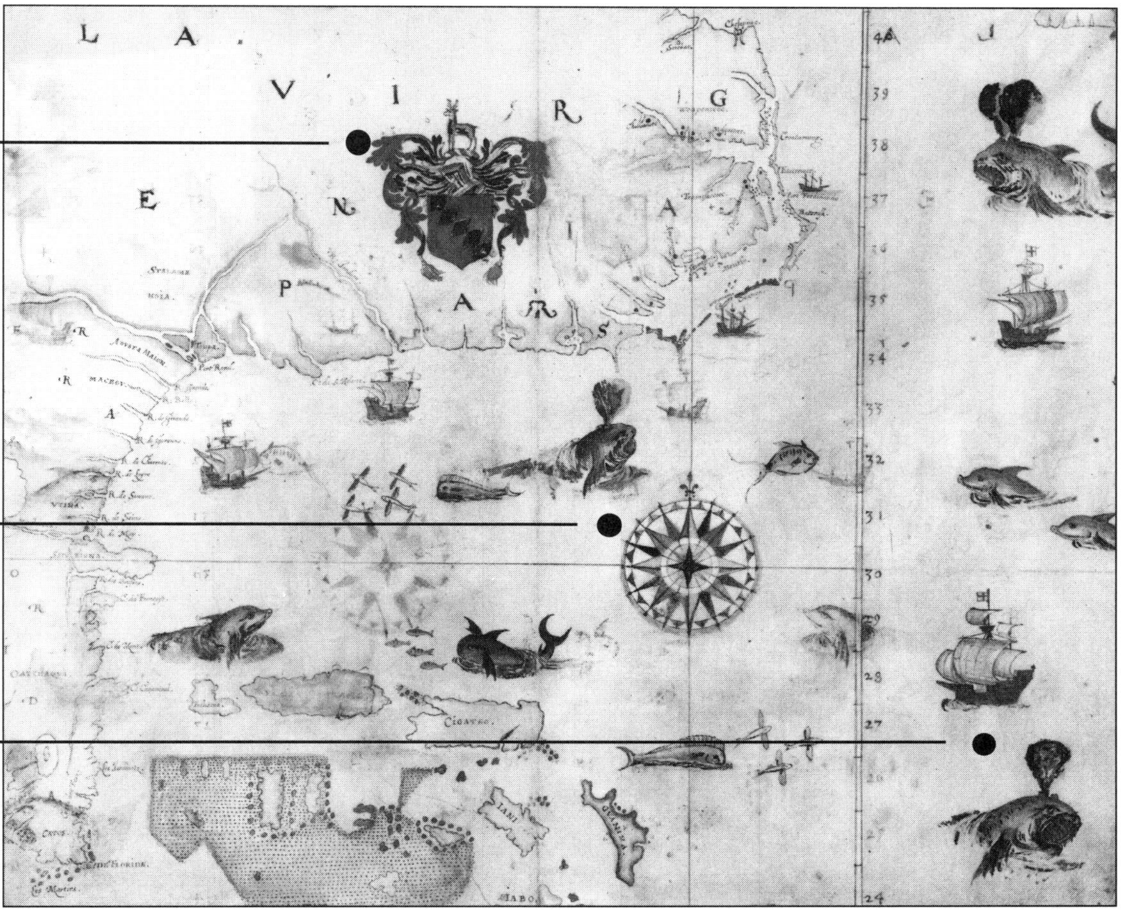

Map of the Virginia Colony by John White

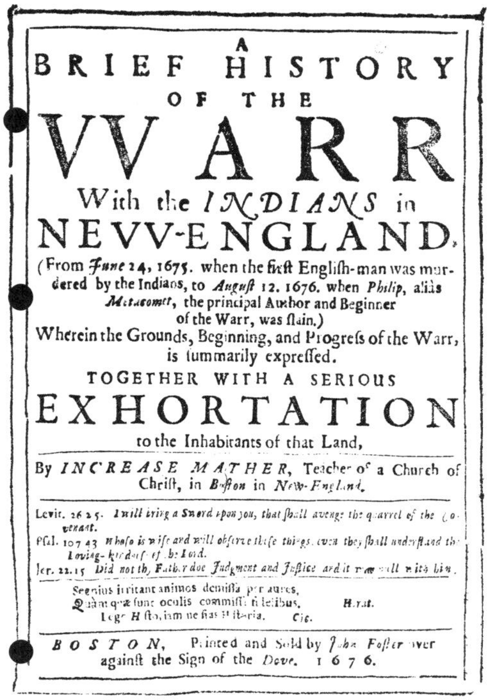

A
BRIEF HISTORY
OF THE
VVARR
With the *INDIANS* in
NEVV-ENGLAND,
(From *June* 24, 1675. when the first English-man was mur-
dered by the Indians, to *August* 12. 1676. when *Philip*, alias
Metacomet, the principal Author and Beginner
of the Warr, was slain.)
Wherein the Grounds, Beginning, and Progress of the Warr,
is summarily expressed.
TOGETHER WITH A SERIOUS
EXHORTATION
to the Inhabitants of that Land,

By *INCREASE MATHER*, Teacher of a Church of
Christ, in *Boston* in *New-England.*

Levit. 26 25. I will bring a Sword upon you, that shall avenge the quarrel of the Co-
venant.
Psal. 107 43 Whoso is wise and will observe these things, even they shall understand the
Loving-kindness of the Lord.
Jer. 22. 15 Did not thy Father doe Judgment and Justice and it was well with him.

Segnius irritant animos demissa per aures,
Quam quæ sunt oculis commissa fidelibus,   *Horat.*
Lege Historiam ne fias Historia.   *Cic.*

BOSTON,   Printed and Sold by *John Foster* over
against the Sign of the *Dove.*   1 6 7 6.

Title page of A Brief History of the
Warr with the Indians of New-
England, *by Increase Mather, 1676*

AMERICA

T' AMSTERDAM

By Jacob van Meurs, Plaetsnyder en Boeckverkooper op de Keysers graft in de Stadt Meurs. 1671.

Introduction

This woodcut from a 1537 book printed in Lubeck, Germany, portrays Christopher Columbus (standing) and a friend in search of the New World. The ship's design would have been considered primitive by Columbus.

The frontispiece from Jacob van Meurs' America (1671) depicts New Amsterdam (later New York) as a strange and beautiful new world. Native Americans wearing exaggerated costumes bear exotic goods and animals while the Europeans (in background on right and left) look on.

In 1503 Amerigo Vespucci wrote a letter that shook his world. Vespucci, an Italian merchant and adventurer, had just returned from an arduous trip across the Atlantic and, as he did after every voyage, he sent a report to his sponsors in Florence. With his usual flair, Vespucci described his travels to distant, exotic places, which had been entirely unknown to Europeans until Christopher Columbus's voyage of 1492. "I have found a continent more densely peopled and abounding in animals than our Europe or Asia or Africa," Vespucci announced. While Columbus believed these lands were actually part of Asia, Vespucci had come to think differently. "These we may rightly call a new world," he insisted, "because our ancestors had no knowledge of them, and it will be a matter wholly new to all those who hear about them."

"Wholly new" indeed! Imagine a NASA space shuttle accidentally stumbling onto a previously unobserved planet in our own solar system, only to find it populated by other humans, and you'll come close to imagining what it meant when Vespucci said "our ancestors had no knowledge of them." Or, to get some idea of what the arrival of European ships must have meant to the native inhabitants of this world, imagine alien spaceships making a spectacular landing on the Empire State Building in Manhattan, with men in Star Fleet uniforms peeping out of the portals.

What Amerigo Vespucci called "a new world" was of course new only to people who had never known of its existence, just as Manhattan would seem entirely new only to explorers from another planet. To the people who were then living in the lands Vespucci visited, Europe was the new world. Nevertheless, journeys like those made by Vespucci, and the "age of encounters" that began with Columbus's voyage in 1492, forever altered our world. The legacies of that age—the emigration of huge numbers of Europeans across the Atlantic, the decimation of the Native American population, the growth of European colonial powers, and the forced removal of millions of Africans to the Americas—continue to shape who we are today.

On the Turtle's Back

Long before Vespucci, well before Columbus, and long, really, before anyone, the world began on a turtle's back. According to an ancient Iroquois legend, the world began when a spirit being fell out of the sky and landed on a turtle's back. As this Sky Woman fell to earth, birds flew up to meet her and Turtle volunteered to offer her a dry place to land. There, on Turtle's back, Sky Woman and her descendants built the world.

Creation stories like the tale of Sky Woman are just one part of the rich cultural heritage of the indigenous peoples of North America. In 1492, humans had been living in North America—on the turtle's back—for between 10,000 and 30,000 years. Their ancestors had gradually traveled here through the land of Beringia, which had once connected Alaska to northeastern Asia. By 1492, the many peoples of North America spanned the continent, forming vastly different cultures and communities, speaking hundreds of different languages. Some lived by fishing, others by hunting, still others by planting crops. Some built wooden or thatched houses; others designed elaborate buildings in the sides of cliffs or dazzling cities in lowland valleys. Among settled agricultural societies such as the Aztecs, Mayas, and Incas, complex civilizations developed with elaborate religious traditions, art forms, and political structures.

In Vespucci's 1503 report on his voyage he wrote, "We found in those parts such a multitude of people as nobody could enumerate." Historians, too, have found it difficult to calculate the native population of the Americas before contact with Europe. Estimates range as high as 100 million and as low as less than half that number. (At the time, the combined population of all of Europe was about 70 million.) Central and South America were then far more densely populated than North America. Still, the

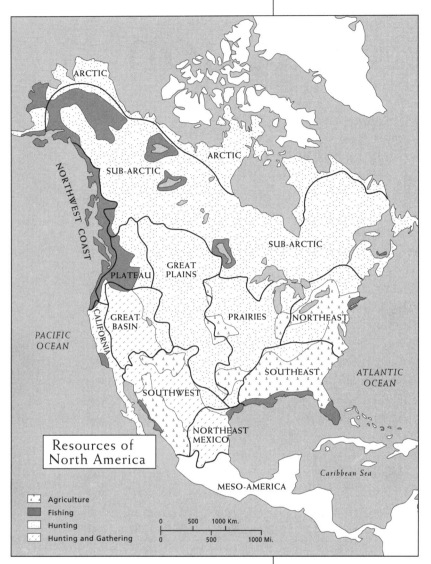

Native American groups living in different regions had developed their own habits and customs by the time the Europeans first arrived. Those living along the coast, for example, depended on fish as a source of food, while those living in fertile areas grew crops.

We Human Beings are the first, and we are the eldest and the greatest. These parts and countries were inhabited and trod upon by the Human Beings before there were any Axe-Makers [Europeans].

—Sadekanaktie, an Iroquois, or Onondaga (1694)

native population of what is now the United States and Canada was probably between 7 and 18 million.

All Native American peoples (who came to be called "Indians" because Columbus thought he had arrived in the Indies), were vulnerable to foreign diseases like smallpox, measles, typhoid fever, and influenza, from which they had been isolated for thousands of years and for which they thus had no biological immunity. European contagion inevitably led to terrifying epidemics. Eight million people, or about one-third of the population of Central Mexico, died within ten years of the arrival of Spanish soldiers and explorers. Europeans and Indians alike, neither of whom understood how disease was transmitted, were prone to interpret these epidemics as supernatural in their causes. One Spanish soldier believed God was on the Spaniards' side, for "when the Christians were exhausted from war, God saw fit to send the Indians smallpox." Meanwhile, an English colonist in seventeenth-century Pennsylvania observed that the local Indians had "a superstition that as many Indians must die each year, as the number of Europeans that newly arrive." Yet Indians did not die only from disease: many were killed in brutal wars of conquest, or died of abuse and torture at the hands of Europeans.

The decimation of the Native American population was among the chief reasons Europeans began forcibly transporting Africans to the Americas, beginning in the early 1500s. Early European explorers and colonists, especially the Portuguese and the Spanish, developed intensely exploitative labor systems for their colonial ventures. Initially, they forced the Indians to work in their fields and mines. But since the native population was so vulnerable to Old World diseases, Europeans soon began bringing African men, women, and children to the colonies to do this work. Unlike Indians, Africans had already been exposed to Old World diseases. Moreover, they had developed considerable immunity to tropical diseases, like malaria and yellow fever, that plagued Europeans in the New World. Africans were taken from their homes on the western coast of Africa and across the Atlantic on slave ships. Perhaps 12 to 20 million Africans were thus brought to the Americas. During the age of encounters, more Africans arrived in the New World than Europeans.

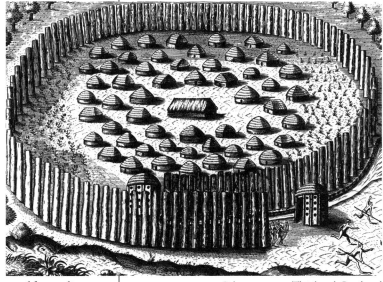

Belgian engraver Théodore de Bry based this view of a typical northeastern Indian village—with a "town hall" at the center—on descriptions by a French explorer. Because few accounts or artifacts from Native Americans themselves exist, historians are often forced to rely on European interpretations.

Do not believe that there exists anything more honourable to our or the preceding age than the invention of the printing press and the discovery of the new world; two things which I always thought could be compared, not only to Antiquity, but to immortality.

—Lazzaro Buonamico (1539)

Why Europe?

Why did Europe "discover" the Americas and not the reverse? The Mayan Indians, after all, made frequent voyages in the Caribbean Sea and had enough knowledge of astronomy to navigate the oceans as early as A.D. 300. And why was it Europeans—rather than Asians, or Arabs, or Africans—who explored the uncharted parts of the globe? During the Middle Ages, China was the richest country in the world and a formidable sea power. The Chinese had invented the compass and, by the time of Columbus's 1492 voyage, possessed both extensive maps and a fleet of "junks," some of the most reliable ships in the world. Meanwhile, northern African and Arab traders had a knowledge of geography and astronomy that surpassed that of Europe, and their ships, known as dhows, dominated the Indian Ocean.

One answer to the question "why Europe?" is that, while other world cultures had ample technology for ocean exploration, none were interested in doing it. The Mayas ruled over an abundant empire that lacked few resources; in a sense, their own self-sufficiency made the idea of travel uncompelling. And, by the second half of the 15th century, the Chinese had retreated from seagoing exploration after having become convinced that the rest of the world was populated only by barbaric and uncivilized peoples. Finally, Arab exploration was reigned in by the dictates of the Koran, the central religious text of Islam, which ordered Muslims not to journey beyond the Mediterranean.

Europe expanded across the Atlantic not because of technological superiority but because of its outward-looking cultural orientation. Many European cultures had long traditions of travel and exploration, dating most importantly to the Crusades to the Holy Land of

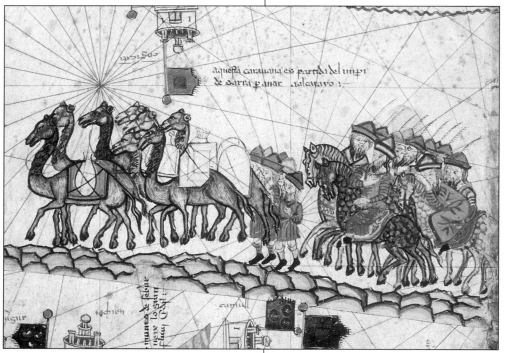

A scene from the Catalan Atlas shows Marco Polo's caravan crossing Asia on the way back from China. Camels carry goods; the passengers ride on horses. The Europeans were determined to expand their world, but the Chinese were less interested in "discovering" other cultures and lands, despite their technological advances and large fleets.

the Roman Catholic Church and the trading ventures of explorers like Marco Polo, who journeyed to China in the late 13th century. Western Europe's religious imperative to spread Christianity, its desire to accumulate wealth through trade, and its increasing population pressures inspired its people to travel beyond its borders.

Dealing with the Documents

In 1503, the report Amerigo Vespucci sent home to Florence proved so fascinating that it was published that year as a book called *Mundus Novus*, or New World. By 1529, *Mundus Novus* had been translated into eight languages and printed in 60 separate editions. (It was so widely read, especially in Germany, that a German mapmaker, Martin Waldseemüller, decided to name the "new world" after its most popular chronicler. In 1507, Waldseemüller engraved a map on which he labeled the new lands "America," and the name stuck.) Because Vespucci was a prolific writer and lived in an age and in a place where writing could be rapidly duplicated (thanks to the recent invention of a printing press with movable type), historians interested in studying Vespucci can pore over pages and pages of original documents to learn about what he thought and did. Libraries all over the world own copies of *Mundus Novus*, and many other important documents from Vespucci's lifetime—letters, portraits, engravings, maps—have survived in historical archives.

Meanwhile, the people Vespucci and other Europeans met in the Americas have left many fewer written documents. Only three Native American cultures—the Aztecs, the Mayas, and the Incas—had their own writing systems and, tragically, European invaders destroyed many of these cultures' written and other artifacts. As a result, precious few documents written by the Indians themselves survive today, especially from the period before 1700. To understand how Indians thought and acted, historians often have to rely on accounts written not by Indians but by Europeans. In other words, to understand the people Vespucci met, we must read not their own accounts (since none exist) but Vespucci's. What this amounts to, of course, is hearing only one side of the argument (and, often enough, hearing it from someone who has little or no understanding of or sympathy for the other side). The possibilities for inaccuracies in European documents about Native Americans or Africans are very great. Like most storytellers, European writers often exaggerated, so when Vespucci writes, "They

The Koran prohibited Arab sailors from venturing beyond the Mediterranean world. Even so, they built sturdy ships, stitching planks together with coconut fiber. Here, the stitching is visible just above the waves.

The discovery of America, and that of a passage to the East Indies by the Cape of Good Hope, are the two greatest and most important events recorded in the history of mankind.

—Adam Smith,
The Wealth of Nations (1776)

Men of strange appearance have come across the great water. They have landed on our island [North America]. Their skins are white like snow, and on their faces long hair grows. These people have come across the great water in wonderfully large canoes which have great white wings like those of a giant bird. The men have long and sharp knives, and they have long black tubes which they point at birds and animals. The tubes make a smoke that rises into the air just like the smoke from our pipes. From them come fire and such terrific noise that I was frightened, even in my dream.

—Ojibwa prophet

live one hundred and fifty years," we must be suspicious. And, since Vespucci did not know the language spoken by the Indians he met, when he claims that "they live together without king, without government, and each is his own master," we must wonder how he knows.

To see just how distorted a picture explorers like Vespucci may have painted of native life, take a look at this description—written not by a European explorer during the age of encounters, but by a historian writing in the 1980s:

> Not long after, they tooke me to one of their great Counsells, where many of the generalitie were gathered in greater number than ever I had seen before. And they being assembled about a great field of open grass, a score of their greatest men ran out upon the field, adorned each in brightly hued jackets and breeches, with letters cunningly woven upon their Chestes, and wearinge hats upon their heads, of a sort I know not what. One of their chiefs stood in the midst and would at his pleasure hurl a white ball at another chief, whose attire was of a different colour, and whether by chance or artyfice I know not the ball flew exceeding close to the man yet never injured him, but sometimes he would strike att it with a wooden club and so gieveing it a hard blow would throw down his club and run away. Such actions proceeded in like manner at length too tedious to mention, but the generalitie waxed wroth, with great groaning and shoutinge, and seemed withall much pleased.

What is the writer describing? A religious ritual? A scene of ceremonial torture? Read the account more closely. Does anything sound familiar?

Although this account is modeled after the writing style of an important seventeenth-century English colonist, Captain John Smith (of Pocahontas fame), it was not written by Smith, nor does it describe 17th-century Algonquian Indians in Virginia. Instead, this description was written by a present-day historian trying to imagine how John Smith would report on a baseball game between the Boston Red Sox and the New York Yankees! Someone who knew nothing about baseball and did not know the language of the players and spectators might indeed have written a similarly confused account of a game at Fenway Park. When reading documents written by Europeans about Native Americans or Africans, then, remember that what a European writer describes as "striking at a white ball with a wooden club" might really be "grounding out to shortstop."

Chapter One

Mapping the World

People have always made maps, whether drawn on paper, etched into bark, or traced in the sand. However they are made, maps are an attempt to describe the world or some part of it, but maps do other things, too: they delineate nations, mark off territory, and characterize a land's inhabitants. Sometimes, deliberately or not, maps lie. Maps can include places that don't exist, can erase whole cultures or continents, and frequently distort sizes, shapes, and directions. Maps are not reality, they merely try to represent it. Because maps are representations, the way a mapmaker chooses to depict the world often tells us as much about the mapmaker as it does about the places shown on the map. In the broadest sense, maps are windows into whole systems of knowledge and belief: through them one can chart the evolution of navigational, geographical, and cartographic knowledge and trace the history of religious, political, and cultural ideas.

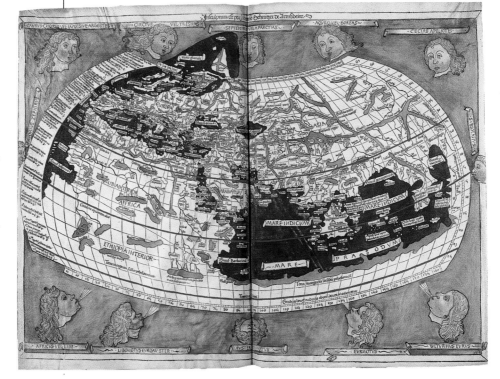

The world according to Ptolemy, an ancient Greek astronomer, reproduced in the Ulm edition of the Geography, *published in Germany in 1482. Ptolemy introduced a new idea in map projection—representing the spherical world on a flat piece of paper. The map's curved edges attempt to keep distortion of geographic areas to a minimum.*

Ptolemy's Revolution

Claudius Ptolemy, a Greek astronomer in Alexandria, Egypt, who lived in the second century A.D., made important contributions to the science of cartography that were lost to Europe during the Middle Ages. In the late 15th century, when Ptolemy's work was rediscovered and printed widely in Europe, it sparked a revolution in mapmaking. The advent of map printing helped make Ptolemy's the dominant world map after 1475. No maps made by him survive, but Renaissance mapmakers used his calculations to make Ptolemaic maps.

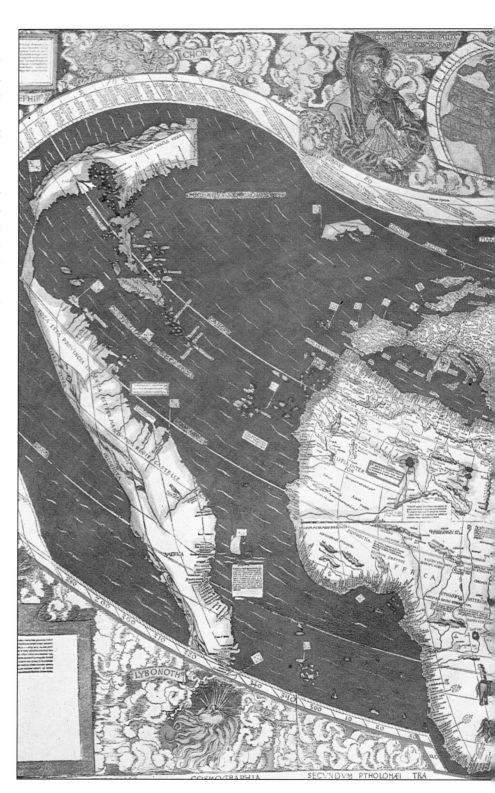

Martin Waldseemüller's 1507 world map shows Ptolemy (upper left) presiding over a Ptolemaic map of the so-called Old World, while Amerigo Vespucci (upper right) stands next to the New World he claimed to have discovered. The new world is labeled "America" in the lower left corner near the southern tip of South America, and was the first map of the world to name the new continents after Vespucci. Although Waldseemüller later attributed the founding of South America to Christopher Columbus, the name "America" stuck.

The Christian World

Maps from the centuries preceding Europe's encounter with the Americas express the wholly religious worldview that dominated medieval Europe. Most world maps from this period contain very little geographic information and are instead filled with religious symbols and icons. T-O maps, named for their depiction of the earth as a round disk often surrounded by a circular ocean, represented a Christian view of the world.

In this 7th-century T-O map by Archbishop Isidore of Seville, Spain, the T forms a cross, to represent Christianity, and the division of the world into three parts echoes the trinity of the medieval church—Father, Son, and Holy Spirit. Archbishop Isidore's map was widely reproduced in the Middle Ages and in 1472 was the first map to be printed in Europe.

This T-O map divides the world into four parts: Asia (upper left), Arabia (upper right), Africa (lower right), and Europe (lower left). The walled garden at the top—in the region farthest from the known countries around the Mediterranean—represents the Garden of Eden.

Opposite: This 13th-century devotional Psalter Map depicts Jesus Christ standing above the world as its overseer. Medieval mappa mundi *(literally, maps of the world) are based on the older T-O maps (with Jerusalem, the holiest site for Christians, at the center) and are similarly religious in emphasis, but they may occasionally contain more geographical information. Note the small T-O globe in Christ's left hand.*

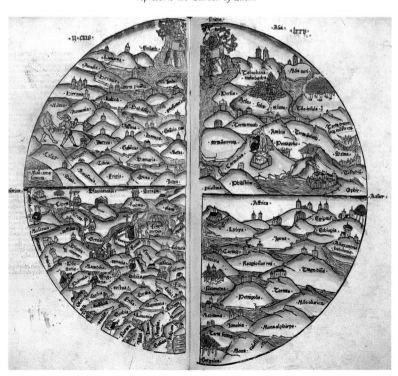

An Expanding World

Maps are among the richest and most revealing documents of the age of encounters. Many are tentative, simple sketches, like Columbus's hastily drawn map of the coast of Hispaniola, made during his second trans-Atlantic voyage in 1493. Others are exquisitely detailed and lavishly decorated, like Willem Blaeu's double-hemisphere map of the world engraved in 1630. Still others are carefully painted on animal skins, like a map made by the Catawba Indians of the Carolinas about 1720. Like all map makers, Columbus, van den Keere, and the Catawba Indian who painted this deerskin map made choices about which details to include, what to ignore, and what to alter when they made their maps. How they made those choices tells us a great deal about how they saw their world and how they wanted others to see it. And, like all maps of the age of encounters, their maps tell the story of a meeting of worlds.

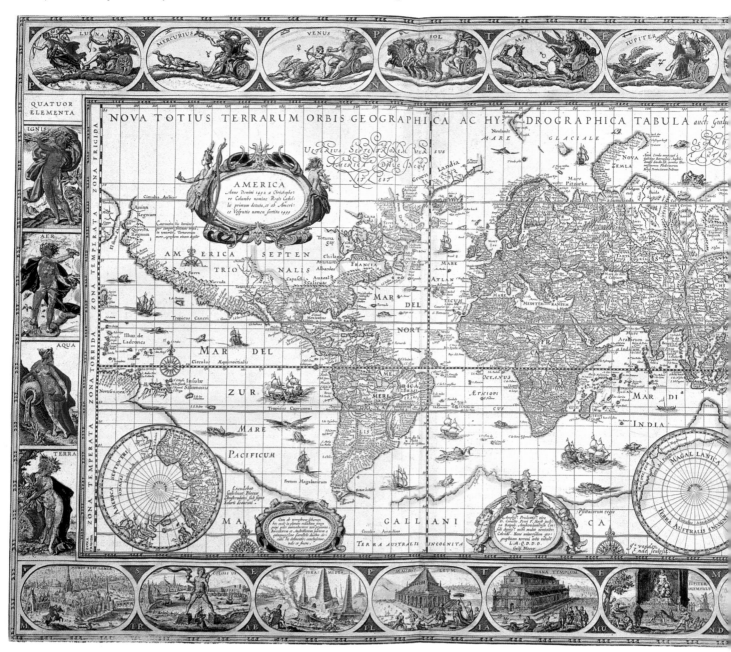

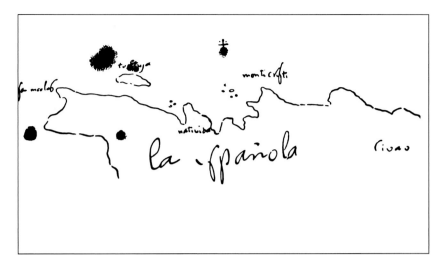

Columbus's map records his "discovery" and, more importantly, documents Spain's "possession" of what Columbus named *La Isla Española*, or the Spanish Isle. Hispaniola had a local name before Columbus arrived, of course, but his map makes no note of it. Nor does it mention the 250,000 people who were living there when he first arrived—no dots or X's mark their settlements, no symbols show their fishing bays.

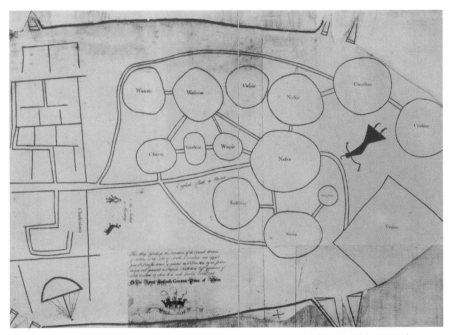

This Catawba map neither documents possession nor celebrates superiority: it records trade and diplomatic relationships. The circles on the map represent Sioux-speaking communities; the square represents the colony of Virginia.

This 1630 world map by Willem Blaeu is perhaps the supreme artifact of the golden age of European mapmaking. Vignettes at the top represent the moon and planets. At left are the elements; at right, the seasons. The seven wonders of the ancient world fill the bottom panels. Unlike Columbus's sketch, Blaeu's map is not particularly useful for navigation or any other practical purpose; it is decorative, intended primarily to celebrate Europe's new global dominance in trade, science, and the arts.

America Emerges

After the voyages of Columbus, Vespucci, and other early explorers, European navigators began mapping the coastal areas of the continents on the other side of the Atlantic. Many maps show a finely detailed outline of the entire eastern coast of North and South America, but the inland areas are left almost entirely empty, except for trees and animals. These maps contributed to the illusion that the world consisted only of the parts of it that Europeans had visited.

Sebastian Münster's 1546 woodcut map was the first printed map of the Western Hemisphere and the first to show North and South America as separate continents. Along with trees, Münster illustrated the Americas with a picture of cannibalism (the pile of bones located in modern Brazil). Images of cannibalism had become a familiar European motif to represent American native life. Münster himself had never been to the Americas and had no actual evidence of the existence of cannibalism among any Native American peoples. The motif, however, reinforced a common European idea about "savage" Indians.

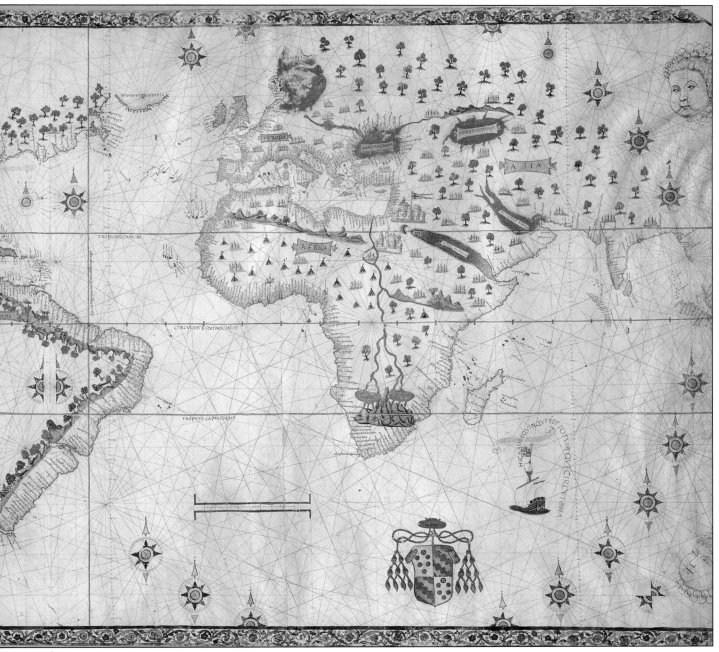

This 1515 Spanish parchment map may have been a gift from Charles V of Spain to Cardinal Giovanni Salviati, whose crest appears in the lower right corner of the map. The delineation of the eastern coast of the Americas is exceptionally accurate compared to contemporary maps. A thin strip of trees and animals inhabit the unexplored lands of the Americas' interior. A small, detailed layout of the city of Tenochtitlán, the Aztec capital, appears just inside the gulf coastline of present-day Mexico.

Giovanni de Rossi's 1687 map entitled "L'America Settentrionale" is a slightly edited version of an earlier map drawn by French mapmaker Guillaume Sanson. The map is color coded to indicate which European power has laid claim to the land. The political divisions on Rossi's map are distinctly pro-French, with Nova Francia embracing most of the eastern half of North America. England is given only upper Labrador and Hudson Bay, New England, and Virginia, while Connecticut, New York, New Jersey, and Delaware are implicitly given to the Dutch and Swedes, though neither seriously claimed the areas at the time. In addition, France gets "French Florida" (part of South Carolina and Georgia). On the west coast, Rossi includes a detailed rendering of California as an island, a common misconception of the time period. Alaska and Canada are shown here to belong to Denmark.

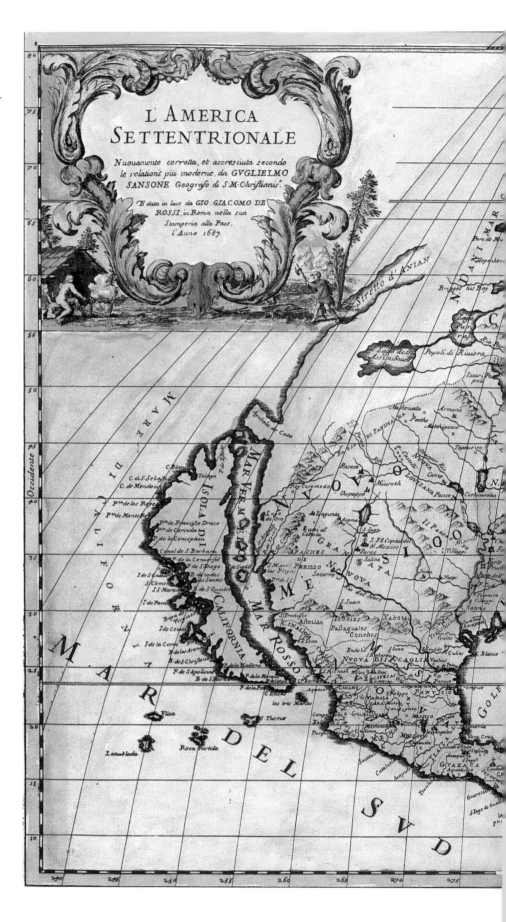

Captain John Smith, who helped establish the early English colony of Jamestown in Virginia, would never have been able to make this map without assistance from the local Algonquian Indians, the Powhatans. As he himself wrote, "In which Mappe observe this, that as far as you see the little Crosses on rivers, mountaines, or other places, have been discovered; the rest was had by information of the Savages, and are set downe according to their instructions."

Vanishing Maps

Often, Indian maps were made on perishable materials—drawn in the sand, or carved into animal hides or tree bark. As a result, many maps made by Native Americans have not survived. Maps made by the Aztecs of Mexico are some of the rare examples that do survive, though many Aztec maps were destroyed by the Spanish. European settlers, colonizers, and conquerors relied heavily on Native American geographical knowledge in making their own maps. But, like the maps of medieval and early modern Europe, many Native American maps are more concerned with a religious worldview.

Like a European T-O map, this Aztec map of the world is a symbolic representation, depicting the five parts of the world and the gods who live in them. The Aztecs were accomplished cartographers and also created maps for route locating, surveying, and town planning. These maps were often reproduced by the conquering Spanish.

Lines and Circles

The few native maps that do survive are often strikingly different from those made by Europeans, at least after the late 15th century. In the age of encounters, Europeans and Euroamericans usually used maps to document their possession of certain territories. As a result, European maps are most concerned with drawing lines to separate one person's property from that of another, or one nation's boundaries from its neighbors'. However, traditional Native American cultures did not subscribe to the idea that land can be "owned" in the European sense, so that most native maps demonstrate little concern with the boundaries of territories. Instead, native maps document not control of territory but relationships between peoples.

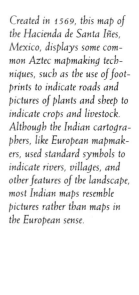

Created in 1569, this map of the Hacienda de Santa Iñes, Mexico, displays some common Aztec mapmaking techniques, such as the use of footprints to indicate roads and pictures of plants and sheep to indicate crops and livestock. Although the Indian cartographers, like European mapmakers, used standard symbols to indicate rivers, villages, and other features of the landscape, most Indian maps resemble pictures rather than maps in the European sense.

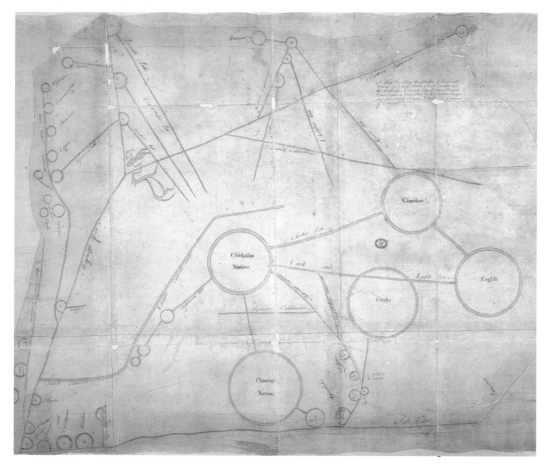

This 1737 Alabama Indian map, copied from the deerskin original, depicts Chickasaw villages (indicated by circles) and the relationships between them (indicated by the straight lines).

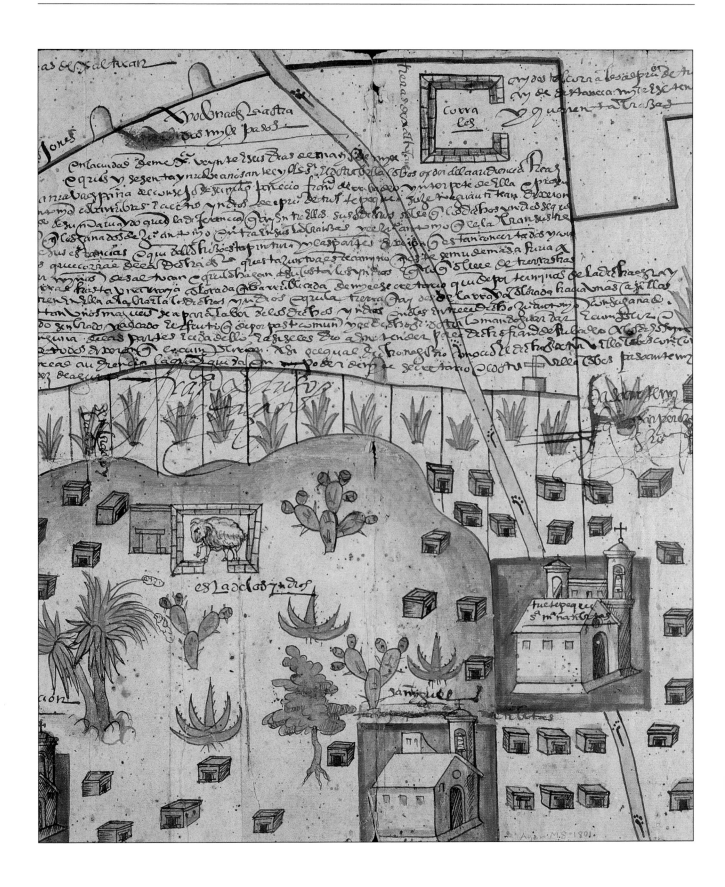

Windows into the Past

Maps are fascinating windows into the past, and, especially, into the age of encounters, when the world was changing so dramatically for both European and Native American peoples. Maps might not tell us too much about how Europe and the Americas actually looked, but what they do tell us about is perhaps even more valuable: maps tell us how people saw their world.

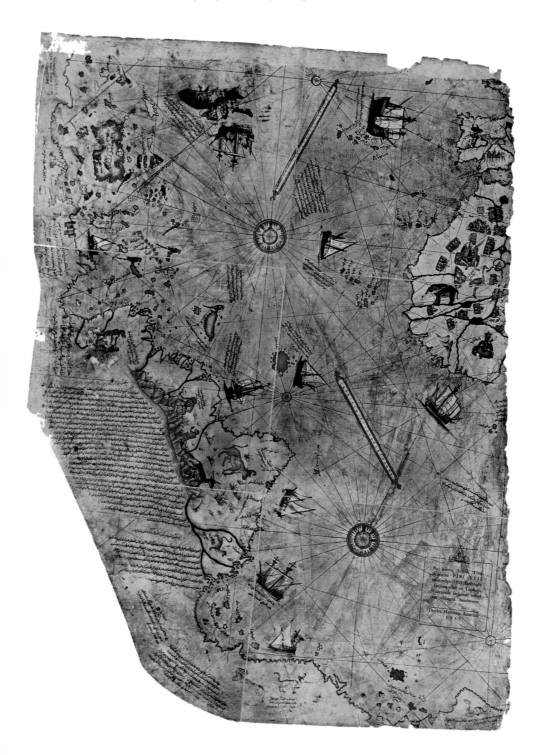

Piri Reis was a Turkish navigator and cartographer. His 1513 map of the Caribbean Sea and the coast of Brazil (left) is most likely based on a chart drawn by Christopher Columbus. Historians believe that Columbus's chart belonged to a Spanish sailor who was captured by Reis's uncle, a ship captain. Reis acquired the chart and incorporated it into his own map. The map shows 42 place names in the New World; nearly all of them can be identified with places explored and named by Columbus. In a long note in the margin (lower left) Piri Reis gives a narrative account of Columbus's first three voyages. The cartographer decorated his map with pictures of several varieties of ships and also of mythical creatures, such as a unicorn roaming the Brazilian forest. In all, the Piri Reis map is not only a masterpiece of cartography, but is also a unique record of how Columbus described his own voyages.

Chapter Two

First Encounters

Amerigo Vespucci found Indians shocking. "All of both sexes go about naked, covering no part of their bodies," he wrote, and their skin is "in color verging upon reddish." But if Europeans were astonished by Indians' nakedness and by the color of their skin, Indians were equally amazed by the newcomers' strange appearance. As the Aztecs in Mexico observed of the Spanish, "Their bodies were everywhere covered; only their faces appeared. They were very white; they had chalky faces; they had yellow hair, though the hair of some was black. Long were their beards; they also were yellow."

Encounters between peoples who had not previously known of one another's existence were bound to be profoundly unsettling. Not surprisingly, at first meeting they usually found each other bizarre in the extreme. Even as late as 1709, the Englishman John Lawson could write, "Their way of Living is so contrary to ours that neither we nor they can fathom one another's Designs and Methods." Europeans and Native Americans were quick to notice each other's differences. In 1584, Arthur Barlowe found that the Algonquians who greeted the English at Roanoke Island "wondred mervelously when we were amongest them, at the whiteness of our skinnes, ever coveting to touch our breastes and to view the same." But, while some Native Americans were awed by Europeans—at least at first—the reverse was not true; Europeans usually regarded the Indians with pity or disgust rather than admiration.

Many Native American peoples lived in small bands, tribes, or confederacies and, while they had much contact with neighboring communities, their neighbors were not likely to be very different from themselves. European peoples, on the other hand, had a long tradition of travel and exploration—to Africa and the Far East, especially— through which they met men and women extraordinarily different from themselves. Within Europe's cultural traditions, especially those

Each man calls barbarism whatever is not his own practice. . . . Barbarians are no more marvelous to us than we are to them, nor for better cause.

—Michel de Montaigne, "Of Cannibals" (1580)

[handwritten: How did they view each other and what conditioned those views?]

derived from the Bible, people who were different were considered by definition inferior: "savage" (fierce and beastlike), "heathen" (un-Christian), and "barbaric" (speaking strange languages). Meanwhile, the most powerful Native American convention for understanding dramatically different people was their concept of spiritual beings, or gods inhabiting the natural world. In other words, Europeans were culturally predisposed to see others as savages, while Native Americans were inclined to view strangers as gods. European writers no doubt greatly exaggerated this inclination, however, since they were eager to confirm their own view that Indians would quickly recognize the supposed superiority of European culture.

The first encounters of Europeans and North Americans were often terrifyingly brutal. The attitudes the Europeans brought to America about the "inferiority" of the indigenous peoples often led them to quickly kill, capture, or enslave the natives they found. But second encounters could be even more brutal. Once Europeans and Native Americans began to know one another, conflicts between their cultures often only grew. Many Europeans in the New World expected Native Americans to subject themselves willingly to European monarchs and voluntarily adopt the trappings of European culture and customs. But the Indian peoples had their own political systems and cultural loyalties and, while they were often intrigued by the goods and technologies introduced by the Europeans, few Indians were interested in simply abandoning their own ways. Quite the contrary; many felt that if anyone should adapt, it ought to be the Europeans. As one Wicomesse Indian said to the English governor of Maryland in 1633, "Since that you are heere strangers and come into our Countrey, you should rather confine yourselves to the Customes of our Countrey, than impose yours upon us."

[handwritten: What led to violent conflicts after peaceful initial encounters?]

Prophecies, Plans, and Fantasies

The Indians often understood the arrival of Europeans to be the fulfillment of prophecy. The Taínos, native to Hispaniola, told the Spaniards who accompanied Columbus that they had long expected that "within a few years a race of men wearing clothes would land in the island and would overthrow their religious rites and ceremonies, massacre their children, and make them slaves." Other native stories predicted the arrival of "floating islands"—European ships—and warned that tragedies of disease and conquest would

follow in the ships' wakes. Meanwhile, Europeans brought their own prophecies, predictions, and fantasies to encounters with new peoples.

The Aztecs of central Mexico witnessed a series of ominous signs—furious fires, terrifying lightning bolts, and strange birds—in the years before the Spanish first arrived, at the beginning of the 16th century. They recorded these omens in their native language, Nahuatl. Montezuma, an Aztec leader, consulted his advisors to learn how to understand the warnings.

The first bad omen: Ten years before the Spaniards first came here, a bad omen appeared in the sky. It was like a flaming ear of corn, or a fiery signal, or the blaze of daybreak; it seemed to bleed fire, drop by drop, like a wound in the sky. It was wide at the base and narrow at the peak, and it shone in the very heart of the heavens....

When it first appeared, there was great outcry and confusion. The people clapped their hands against their mouths; they were amazed and frightened, and asked themselves what it could mean.

The second bad omen: The temple of Huitzilopochtli burst into flames. It is thought that no one set it afire, that it burned down of its own accord. . . .

The third bad omen: A temple was damaged by a lightning-bolt. This was the temple of Xiuhtecuhtli, which was built of straw, in the place known as Tzonmolco. It was raining that day, but it was only a light rain or drizzle, and no thunder was heard. Therefore the lightning-bolt was taken as an omen. The people said: "The temple was struck by a blow from the sun."

The fourth bad omen: Fire streamed through the sky while the sun was still shining. It was divided into three parts. It flashed out from where the sun sets and raced straight to where the sun rises, giving off a shower of sparks like a red-hot coal. When the people saw its long train streaming through the heavens, there was a great outcry and confusion, as if they were shaking a thousand little bells.

The fifth bad omen: The wind lashed the water until it boiled. It was as if it were boiling with rage, as if it were shattering itself in its frenzy. It began from far off, rose high in the air and dashed against the walls of the houses. . . .

Aztecs in Mexico meet the arriving Spaniards and marvel at their possessions. Although Europeans generally considered the Indians to be barbarians or savages, the Indians were awed by the newcomers with their powerful weapons and wealth of goods.

The sixth bad omen: The people heard a weeping woman night after night. She passed by in the middle of the night, wailing and crying out in a loud voice: "My children, we must flee far away from this city!" At other times she cried: "My children, where shall I take you?"

The seventh bad omen: A strange creature was captured in the nets. The men who fish the lakes caught a bird the color of ashes, a bird resembling a crane. They brought it to Montezuma in the Black House. This bird wore a strange mirror in the crown of its head. The mirror was pierced in the center like a spindle whorl, and the night sky could be seen in its face. The hour was noon, but the stars and the *mamalhuaztli* could be seen in the face of that mirror. Montezuma took it as a great and bad omen when he saw the stars and the *mamalhuaztli*.

But when he looked at the mirror a second time, he saw a distant plain. People were moving across it, spread out in ranks and coming forward in great haste. They made war against each other and rode on the backs of animals resembling deer.

Montezuma called for his magicians and wise men and asked them: "Can you explain what I have seen? Creatures like human beings, running and fighting . . . !" But when they looked in the mirror to answer him, all had vanished away, and they saw nothing.

The eighth bad omen: Monstrous beings appeared in the streets of the city: deformed men with two heads but only one body. They were taken to the Black House and shown to Montezuma; but the moment he saw them, they all vanished away.

A Micmac Indian tradition tells of how a young woman's dream predicted the arrival of French missionaries and traders to the Great Lakes region—missionaries who seemed, at first, more like bears than men.

When there were no people in this country but Indians, before white people were known, a young woman had a strange dream. She dreamed that a small island came floating in toward the land. On the island were tall trees and living beings. Among them was a man dressed in garments made of rabbit skins.

In those days it was the custom, when anyone had an unusual dream, to consult the wise men of the tribe, especially the prophets and magicians. So the girl related her dream and asked what it meant. The wise men pondered but could make nothing of it. On the second day after the girl's dream, however, something happened that explained it.

When they got up that morning, they saw what seemed to be a small island that had drifted near to the land and become fixed there. There were trees on the island, and what seemed to be a number of bears were crawling about on the branches.

All the Micmac men seized their bows and arrows and spears, and rushed down to the shore to shoot the bears. But they stopped in surprise when they saw that the creatures were not bears but men. And what had seemed to be a small island with trees was really a large boat with long poles rising above it. While the Indians stood watching, some of the men on the ship lowered a strangely built canoe into the water. Several of them jumped into it and paddled ashore.

Among those in the strange canoe was a man dressed in white. As he came toward the shore, he made signs of friendship, by raising his hand toward heaven. He talked to the Indians in an earnest manner, in a language they did not understand.

Now people began to question the girl about her dream: "Was it an island like this that you saw in your dream?" "Yes." "Is the man in the white robe the one you saw in your dream?" "Yes, he was."

Then some of the prophets and magicians were greatly displeased—displeased because the coming of these strangers to their land had been revealed to a young girl instead of to them. If an enemy had been about to make an attack on them, they could have foreseen it and foretold it by the power of their magic. But of the coming of this white-robed man, who proved to be a priest of a new religion, they knew nothing.

The new teacher gradually won his way into their favor, though the magicians opposed him. The people received his instruction and were baptized. The priest learned their language and gave them the prayer-book written in ornamental mark-writing.

While the Native American peoples prophesied the arrival of Europeans, Europeans fantasized about what awaited them in the lands they hoped to "discover." Some ten years before Columbus made his first voyage, his friend Paolo Pozzi Toscanelli wrote to encourage him. Toscanelli believed Columbus would find "powerful kingdoms" and people eager to become Christians.

I notice thy splendid and lofty desire to sail to the regions of the east by those of the west, as is shown by the chart which I sent you, which would be better shown in the shape of a round sphere; it would please me greatly, should it be understood; and that not only

Columbus's first letter describing his voyage to the New World was immensely popular in Europe. It was printed and published nine times in 1493. By 1500, 20 editions had been printed. As one contemporary of Columbus wrote, "Raise your spirits. . . . Hear about the new discovery!"

is the said voyage possible, but it is sure and certain, and of honor and countless gain, and of the greatest renown among all Christians.

When the said journey occurs, it will be to powerful kingdoms and most noble cities and provinces, most rich in all manner of things in great abundance and very necessary to us, as also in all kinds of spices in great quantity, and of jewels in the largest abundance.

It will also be to the said kings and princes who are very desirous, more than we are, to have dealing and speech with Christians from our parts, for a great number of them are Christians, and also to have speech and dealing with the learned men and men of genius from here, as well in religion as in all the other sciences, because of the great reputation of the empires and administrations of these our parts; for all which things and many others which might be mentioned, I do not wonder that thou who art of great spirit, and the whole nation of the Portuguese, who have always been men noble in all great undertakings, shouldst be seen with heart inflamed and full of desire to put into execution the said journey.

After Columbus returned from his voyage in 1493, Pope Alexander VI issued a bull, or statement of policy, dividing the newfound lands between Spain and Portugal, in the name of the Catholic Church. In the bull, Alexander addresses the Spanish monarchs, Ferdinand and Isabella. As head of the church, Alexander claimed the right to "give, grant, and assign" these lands to Spain and Portugal, provided that none of the territory was already ruled or claimed by a "Christian king or prince." In Alexander's eyes, the fact that these lands were populated only by "barbarous nations" gave him authority over them.

Among other works well pleasing to the Divine Majesty and cherished of our heart, this assuredly ranks highest, that in our times especially the Catholic faith and the Christian religion be exalted and be everywhere increased and spread, that the health of souls be cared for and that barbarous nations be overthrown and brought to the faith itself. . . .

We have indeed learned that you, who for a long time had intended to seek out and discover certain islands and mainlands remote and unknown and not hitherto discovered by others, to the end that you might bring to the worship of our Redeemer and the profession of the Catholic faith their residents and inhabitants, . . . with the wish to fulfill your desire, chose our beloved son, Christopher Columbus . . . to make diligent quest for these remote and unknown mainlands and islands through the sea, where hitherto no one had sailed; and they at length, with divine aid and with the utmost diligence sailing in the ocean sea, discovered certain very remote islands and even mainlands . . . wherein dwell very many peoples living in peace, and, as reported, going unclothed, and not eating flesh. . . .

Wherefore, as becomes Catholic kings and princes, after earnest consideration of all matters, especially of the rise and spread of the Catholic faith, as was the fashion of your ancestors, kings of renowned memory, you have purposed with the favor of divine clemency to bring under your sway the said mainlands and islands with their residents and inhabitants to bring them to the Catholic faith. . . .

In order that you may enter upon so great an undertaking with greater readiness and heartiness endowed with the benefit of our apostolic favor, we . . . give, grant, and assign to you and your heirs and successors . . . all islands and mainlands found and to be found, discovered and to be discovered towards the west and south, by drawing and establishing a line from the Arctic pole, namely the north, to the Antarctic pole, namely the south, no matter whether the said mainlands and islands are found and to be found in the direction of Indian or towards any other quarter, the said line to be distant one hundred leagues towards the west and south from any of the islands commonly known as the Azores and Cape Verde.

With this proviso however that none of the islands and mainlands, found and to be found, discovered and to be discovered, beyond that said line towards the west and south, be in the actual possession of any Christian king or prince up to the birthday of our Lord Jesus Christ just past from which the present year one thousand four hundred and ninety-three begins.

First Impressions

Christopher Columbus's ship's log is one of the most important—and most fascinating—documents in American history. Here are his entries for October 12 and 13, 1492, detailing his first encounters in the Caribbean with the natives of an island called Guanahani by the indigenous Lucayans and renamed San Salvador by Columbus. Historians look at documents like Columbus's log to ask, What was he looking for,

and what did he find? Can we tell from this document what the people of Guanahani thought of Columbus? Because of documents like Toscanelli's, just quoted, we know that Columbus expected to find people "very desirous . . . to have dealing[s] and speech with Christians from our parts." Columbus's expectation that the people he encountered would eagerly embrace Christianity made him unable to appreciate that they already practiced a religion. He came to believe instead that they were "naked," both physically and culturally. And, since Columbus was also looking for great riches, especially gold, he took almost any sign as a clue that gold was near.

Upon Columbus's arrival on a new island, his men begin planting the Christian cross. Sometimes, the native islanders considered the Spaniards, wearing such impressive clothes, to be gods themselves and offered gifts.

Assumes trade not gift giving.

Poor because they are naked

[Friday, October 12, 1492]
I[n] order that they would be friendly to us—because I recognized that they were people who would be better freed [from error] and converted to our Holy Faith by love than by force—to some of them I gave red caps, and glass beads which they put on their chests, and many other things of small value, in which they took so much pleasure and became so much our friends that it was a marvel. Later they came swimming to the ships' launches where we were and brought us parrots and cotton thread in balls and javelins and many other things, and they traded them to us for other things which we gave them, such as small glass beads and bells. In sum, they took everything and gave of what they had very willingly. But it seemed to me that they were a people very poor in everything. All of them go around as naked as their mothers bore them; and the women also, although I did not see more than one quite young girl. And all those that I saw were young people, for none did I see of more than 30 years of age. They are very well formed, with handsome bodies and good faces. Their hair [is] coarse—almost like the tail of a horse—and short. They wear their hair down over their eyebrows except for a little in the back which they wear long and never cut. Some of them paint themselves with black, and they are of the color of the Canarians [i.e., from the Canary Islands], neither black nor white; and some of them paint themselves with white, and some of them with red, and some of them with whatever they find. And some of them

paint their faces, and some of them the whole body, and some of them only the eyes, and some of them only the nose. They do not carry arms nor are they acquainted with them, because I showed them swords and they took them by the edge and through ignorance cut themselves. They have no iron. Their javelins are shafts without iron and some of them have at the end a fish tooth and other things. All of them alike are of good-sized stature and carry themselves well. I saw some who had marks of wounds on their bodie and I made signs to them asking what they were; and they showed me how people from other islands nearby came there and tried to take them, and how they defended themselves; and I believed and believe that they come here from *tierra firme* to take them captive. They should be good and intelligent servants, for I see that they saw very quickly everything that is said to them; and I believe that they would become Christians very easily, for it seemed to me that they had no religion. Our Lord pleasing, at the time of my departure I will take six of them from here to Your Highnesses in order that they may learn to speak.

[Saturday, October 13, 1492]

As soon as it dawned, many of these people came to the beach— all young as I have said, and all of good stature—very handsome people . . . and all of them very wide in the forehead and head, more so than any other race that I have seen so far. And their eyes are very handsome and not small; and none of them are black, but of the color of the Canary Islanders. Nor should anything else be expected since this island is on an east-west line with the island of Hierro in the Canaries. All alike have very straight legs and no belly but are very well formed. They came to the ship with dugouts that are made from the trunk of one tree, like a long boat, and all of one piece, and worked marvelously in the fashion of the land, and so big that in some of them 40 and 45 men came. And others smaller, down to some in which came one man alone. They row with a paddle like that of a baker and go marvelously. And if it capsizes on them they then throw themselves in the water, and they right and empty it with calabashes that they carry. They brought balls of spun cotton and parrots and javelins and other little things that it would be tiresome to write down, and they gave everything for anything that was given to them. I was attentive and labored to find out if there was any gold; and I saw that some of them wore a little piece hung in a hole that they have in their noses. And by signs I was able to understand that, going to the south or rounding the island to the south, there was there a king

Although Christopher Columbus thought the Caribbean islanders were poor and lacked proper clothes and tools, he also found them intelligent and believed they would make quick converts to Christianity.

Gold

From across the Atlantic Ocean, King Ferdinand of Spain sits on his throne and watches Columbus land on Hispaniola, home of the Taíno Indians.

Gold

who had large vessels of it and had very much gold. I strove to get them to go there and later saw that they had no intention of going. I decided to wait until the afternoon of the morrow and then depart for the southwest, for, as many of them showed me, they said there was land to the south and to the southwest and to the northwest and that these people from the northwest came to fight them many times. And so I will go to the southwest to seek gold and precious stones. This island is quite big and very flat and with very green tres and muh water and a very large lake in the middle and without any mountains; and all of it is so green that it is a pleasure to look at it. And these people are very gentle, and because of their desire to have some of our things, and believing that nothing will be given to them without their giving something, and not having anything, they take what they can and then throw themselves into the water to swim. But everything they have they give for anything given to them, for they traded even for pieces of bowls and broken glass cups. . . . [Cotton seems to grow] here on this island, but because of the short time I could not declare this for sure. And also the gold that they wear hung in their noses originates here; but in order not to lose time I want to go to see if I can find the island of Cipango. Now, since night had come, all the Indians went ashore in their dugouts.

Often, when Europeans like Columbus met people with different religions, laws, and political systems, they perceived these differences as absences. For instance, Columbus believed that the Taínos of Hispaniola were heathens, people without religion. As he wrote, "I believe that they would become Christians very easily, for it seemed to me that they had no religion." But, as revealed in his ship's log, many of Columbus's first impressions proved false. In fact, the Taínos had a complex religion that revolved around *zemis*, ornamented icons representing spirits. When strangers arrived, the Taínos first consulted their *zemis*.

Columbus's misunderstanding led to one of the many tragedies that would befall the Taínos. When the Spanish later attempted to introduce Christianity to the Taínos and gave them crucifixes and statues of the Virgin Mary, the Taínos

believed that these too were *zemis* and treated them accordingly: they urinated on the icons and buried them in the fields in a ritual intended to increase the harvests. For this perceived blasphemy these Taínos were summarily executed.

The natives of Hispaniola were much impressed by the arrival of the Spaniards. Formerly two caciques [chiefs] . . . fasted for fifteen days in order to consult with the zemis about the future. This fast having disposed the zemis in their favor, they answered that within a few years a race of men wearing clothes would land in the island and would overthrow their religious rites and ceremonies, massacre their children, and make them slaves. This prophecy had been taken by the younger generation to apply to the cannibals; and thus whenever it became known that the cannibals had landed anywhere, the people took flight without even attempting any resistance. But when the Spaniards landed, the islanders then referred the prophecy to them, as being the people whose coming was announced. And in this they were not wrong, for they are all under the dominion of the Christians, and those who resisted have been killed.

Among Columbus's many misunderstandings about the people he met was the idea long held in Europe that some of them were cannibals. Fears about cannibalism played a role not only in European–Native American encounters but in European–African encounters as well. Many Africans captured and sold as slaves believed that their European captors intended to take them to their own country and eat them. Here is how Olaudah Equiano, an African boy born in what is now Nigeria, described his first sight of Europeans as a young boy in the 1750s. Equiano told this story in an autobiography he wrote in 1789.

The first object which saluted my eyes when I arrived on the coast [of Africa] was the sea, and a slave ship which was then riding at anchor and waiting for its cargo. These filled me with astonishment, which was soon converted into terror when I was carried on board. I was immediately handled and tossed up to see if I were sound by some of the crew, and I was now persuaded that I had gotten into a world of bad spirits and that they were going to kill me. Their complexions too differing so much from ours, their long hair and the language they spoke (which was very different from any I had ever heard) united to confirm me in this belief. Indeed

The Taínos considered a wooden household icon, or zemi, such as this one, to be the representation of a spirit. They consulted the zemis in order to receive prophecies.

such were the horrors of my views and fears at the moment that, if ten thousand worlds had been my own, I would have freely parted with them all to have exchanged my condition with that of the meanest slave in my own country. When I looked round the ship too and saw a large furnace or copper boiling and a multitude of black people of every description chained together, every one of their countenances expressing dejection and sorrow, I no longer doubted my fate; and quite overpowered with horror and anguish, I fell motionless on the deck and fainted.

Gods? Savages?

It is possible that during their early encounters some Native Americans initially believed that the Europeans had supernatural, or spiritual, powers. Columbus himself was amazed that several of the Indians he had taken captive seemed to be "still of the opinion that I come from Heaven, for all the intercourse which they have had with me. They were the first to announce this wherever I went. . . . 'Come! Come! See the men from Heaven!' " But Columbus only poorly understood the language and culture of the people he encountered. He and other Europeans may have instead only imagined that the Indians believed him to be a god. Certainly, other Europeans went to great lengths to convince the natives of their powers. In Mexico, for instance, the Spanish conquistador Hernán Cortés deliberately cultivated this misperception by pretending that he could control the thunder.

Cortés . . . answered [the Indians] . . . that now they deserved to be put to death, they and all the people of their towns, but that as we were the vassals of a great King and Lord named the Emperor Don Carlos . . . that if they were not as well disposed as they said they were, that we would take this course, but that if they were not, some of those Tepustles [iron beings] would jump out and kill them for some of the Tepustles were still angry because they had made war on us. At this moment the order was secretly given to put a match to the cannon which had been loaded, and it went off with such a thunderclap as was wanted, and the ball went buzzing over the hills, and as it was mid-day and very still it made a great noise, and the Caciques [chiefs] were terrified on hearing it. As they had never seen anything like it they believed what Cortés had told them was true.

The Banishment of Yayael

While Columbus perceived the Taínos to be heathens, their belief system included many rich traditions, including the following creation story:

There was a man called Yaya, SPIRIT OF SPIRITS, and no one knew his name. His son was named Yayael, "Son of Yaya." This Yayael was banished for wanting to kill his father. Thus he was banished for four months. Afterwards his father killed him, put his bones in a gourd and hung it from the roof of his house where it hung for some time. It came to pass that one day, desiring to see his son, Yaya said to his wife, "I want to see our son Yayael." This made her happy, and taking down the gourd, she turned it over to see the bones of their son. From it gushed forth many fish, big and small. Seeing that these bones had been turned into fishes, they decided to eat them.

[handwritten margin note: Cortes creates idea of strength of guns as spirits]

When the French explorer Jacques Cartier traveled to the Gulf of St. Lawrence in 1535 he, too, was amazed that the natives he encountered there seemed to believe that the French had supernatural powers: they were eager to touch and be touched by Cartier and his companions. As Cartier observed, "One would have thought Christ had come down to earth to heal them." Yet, later in his travels, Cartier came to realize that "rubbing . . . with the hands" was a local custom when greeting strangers and did not necessarily mean that the Indians believed the French had special powers.

As we drew near to their village, great numbers of the inhabitants came out to meet us and gave us a hearty welcome, according to the custom of the country. And we were led by our guides and those who were conducting us into the middle of the village. . . . And at once all the girls and women of the village, some of whom had children in their arms, crowded about us, rubbing our faces, arms and other parts of the upper portions of our bodies which they could touch, weeping for joy at the sight of us and giving us the best welcome they could. They made signs to us also to be good enough to put our hands upon their babies. After this the men made the women retire, and themselves sat down upon the ground round about us, as if we had been going to perform a miracle play. And at once several of the women came back, each with a four-cornered mat, woven like tapestry, and these they spread upon the ground in the middle of the square, and made us place ourselves upon them. When this had been done, the ruler and chief of this tribe, whom in their language they call Agouhanna, was carried in, seated on a large deer-skin, by nine or ten Indians, who came and set him down upon the mats near the Captain, making signs to use that this was their ruler and chief. . . . This chief was completely paralyzed and deprived of the use of his limbs. When he had saluted the Captain and his men, by making signs which clearly meant that they were very welcome, he showed his arms and his legs to the Captain motioning to him to be good enough to touch them, as if he thereby expected to be cured and healed. On this the Captain set about rubbing his arms and legs with his hands. Thereupon this Agouhanna took the band of cloth he was wearing as a crown and presented it to the Captain. And at once many sick persons, some blind, others with but one eye, others lame or impotent and others again so extremely old that their eyelids hung down to their cheeks, were brought in and set down or laid out near the Captain, in order that he might lay his hands

Cortés and the Aztecs

On rare occasions, Europeans found themselves overwhelmed with awe and admiration of native cultures. When Cortés's soldiers first saw the thriving Aztec city of Tenochtitlán (whose population was over 200,000, larger than any European city of the time), they were astonished with its beauty and cleanliness, especially compared to the squalor of most European cities. One of those soldiers, Bernal Díaz, later described the sight:

We saw the three causeways which led into Mexico . . . and we saw the fresh water that comes from Chapultepec which supplies the city, and we saw the bridges on the three causeways which were built at certain distances apart through which the water of the lake flowed in and out from one side to the other, and we beheld on that great lake a great multitude of canoes, some coming with supplies of food and others returning loaded with cargoes of merchandise; and we saw that from every house of that great city and of all the other cities that were built in the water it was impossible to pass from house to house except by drawbridges which were made of wood or in canoes; and we saw in those cities Cues and oratories like towers and fortresses and all gleaming white, and it was a wonderful thing to behold; then the houses with flat roofs, and on the causeways other small towers and oratories which were like fortresses.

After having examined and considered all that we had seen we turned to look at the great market place and the crowds of people that were in it, some buying and others selling, so that the murmur and hum of their voices and words that they used could be heard more than a league off. Some of the soldiers among us who had been in many parts of the world, in Constantinople, and all over Italy, and in Rome, said that so large a market place and so full of people, and so well regulated and arranged, they had never beheld before.

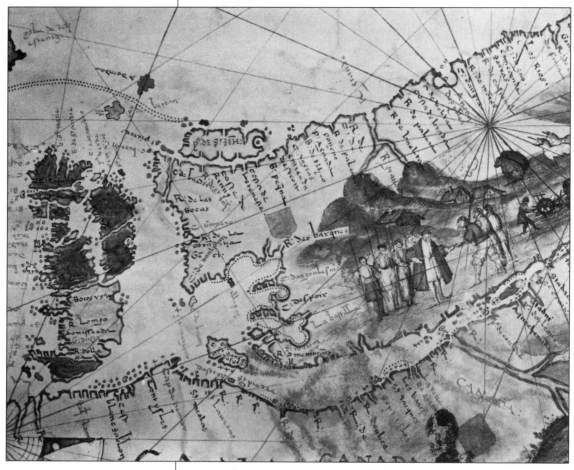

Jacques Cartier, whose portrait most likely appears on this 1542 map, went to North America to look for gold and diamonds for the king of France. Although he failed to find treasure, Cartier's explorations established the basis for France's later claims to Canada.

upon them, so that one would have thought Christ had come down to earth to heal them.

In Rhode Island in the 1640s, the English settler Roger Williams wrote that the products of European technology—ships, books, houses, plows—had convinced the native Narragansetts that the English must be gods, or manitou. Here, as always, there is a problem of translation: does Williams's English word "god" really mean the same thing as the Algonquian word "manitou"?

There is a generall Custome amongst them, at the apprehension of any Excellency in Men, Women, Birds, Beasts, Fish, &c., to cry out *Manittóo*, that is, it is a God, . . . and therefore when they talke amongst themselves of the English ships, and great buildings, of the plowing of their Fields, and especially of Bookes and Letters, they will end thus: *Manittôwock* They are Gods: *Cummanittôo*, you are a God, &c.

If Native Americans were sometimes willing to believe that the Europeans might be more than human, Europeans were often willing to conclude that the Indians were somehow beasts or monsters. Early European notions set important precedents for describing Indians as fantastically primitive people. The European myth of the "savage" Indian meant that Native Americans were either perceived as being naively gentle or fiercely cruel, often as both at once. Here, in two letters, Amerigo Vespucci describes the Indians he encountered as both innocent and vicious. Vespucci, like Columbus, perceived the differentness of native culture as an absence of key cultural elements. To Vespucci it seemed that "they have no laws, and no religious beliefs, but live according to the dictates of nature alone."

[Letter of July 18, 1500]

The first land we found to be inhabited was an island, at ten degrees distant from the equinoctial line. When we arrived at it, we saw on the seashore a great many people who stood looking at us with astonishment. We anchored within about a mile of the land, fitted out the boats, and twenty-two men, well armed, made for land. The people, when they saw us landing, and perceived that we were different from themselves (because they have no beard and wear no clothing of any description, being also of a different color, they being brown and we white), began to be afraid of us, and all ran into the woods. With great exertion, by means of signs, we reassured them, and negotiated with them. We found that they were a race called cannibals, the greater part, or all of whom, live on human flesh.

Your Excellency may rest assured of this fact. They do not eat one another, but navigating with certain barks which they call canoes, they bring their prey from the neighboring islands or countries inhabited by those who are enemies, or of a different tribe from their own. They never eat any women, unless they consider them outcasts. These things we verified in many places where we found similar people.

[Letter of 1502]

We found the region inhabited by a race of people who were entirely naked, both men and women. . . . They have no laws, and no religious belief, but live according to the dictates of nature alone. They know nothing of the immortality of the soul; they have no private property, but every thing in common; they have

Ioan Strada(nus invent.
Theodor Galle fecit, C de Mallery excud.

Vespucci Awakens a Sleeping America

Amerigo Vespucci's portrait of Native Americans as naked and naive came to wield considerable power over Europeans' imaginations. This engraving from the late 16th century is typical of early illustrations of Europe's encounter with America. The picture is full of contrasts. Vespucci, representing Europe, is fully clothed, while a native woman, representing America, is practically naked. Vespucci is standing, "America" lying down; indeed, Vespucci awakens "America" from her slumbers. By the 1570s, representing America as a woman had become a convention, and illustrations like this one had come to reflect Europeans' ideas not only about differences between men and women but also about distinctions between themselves and Indians. To many Europeans, women were by nature both more passive and more emotional than men, who were considered the more assertive, rational sex. Similarly, Europeans considered themselves more active and rational than the natives of the Americas. In short, to many Europeans, men were to women as Europeans were to Indians.

no boundaries of kingdom or province; they obey no king or lord, for it is wholly unnecessary, as they have no laws, and each one is his own master. They dwell together in houses made like huts in the construction of which they use neither iron nor any other metal. This is very remarkable, for I have seen houses two hundred and twenty feet long, and thirty feet wide, built with much skill, and containing five or six hundred people. They sleep in hammocks of cotton, suspended in the air, without any covering; they eat seated upon the ground, and their food consists of the roots of herbs, or fruits and fish. . . .

They are a warlike race, and extremely cruel. . . . The most astonishing thing in all their wars and cruelty was, that we could not find out any reason for them. They made wars against each other, although they had neither kings, kingdoms, nor property of any kind, without any apparent desire to plunder, and without any lust for power, which always appeared to me to be the moving causes of wars and anarchy. When we asked them about this, they gave us no other reason than that they did so to avenge the murder of their ancestors.

Believing that they could save the souls of "heathen" Indians only by converting them to Christianity, Europeans and Euroamericans attempted for centuries to missionize the Indians. Native peoples sometimes accepted Christianity, but just as often rejected it. Some cultures simply incorporated elements of Christian doctrine and ritual into their own religion. Here Red Jacket, an Iroquois leader, criticizes missionaries who had been attempting to convert the Iroquois to Christianity. He delivered this speech in 1828, after the Iroquois had become all too familiar with the Euroamerican idea that the Indians had no religion of their own.

You say that you are sent to instruct us how to worship the Great Spirit agreeably to his mind; and if we do not take hold of the religion which you white people teach, we shall be unhappy hereafter. You say that you are right and we are lost. How do we know this to be true? We understand that your religion is written in a book. If it was intended for us as well as for you, why has not the

Great Spirit given it to us; and not only to us, but why did he not give our forefathers the knowledge of that book, with the means of understanding it rightly? We only know what you tell us about it. How shall we know when to believe, being so often deceived by the white people?

Brother! You say there is but one way to worship and serve the Great Spirit. If there is but one religion, why do you white people differ so much about it? Why do not all agree, as you can all read the book?

Brother! We do not understand these things. We are told that your religion was given to your forefathers, and has been handed down from father to son. We also have a religion which was given to our forefathers, and has been handed down to us their children. We worship that way. It teacheth us to be thankful for all the favors we receive, to love each other, and to be united.

How differently the conquistadores speak about these things, and how far removed they are from Indian practice. And this I believe to be due to the fact that at the time they were not so much concerned with finding things out as with subjecting and acquiring the land. It was also because, coming new to the Indians, they did not know how to ask questions and find things out, for they lacked knowledge of the language; while the Indians, for their part, were too frightened to give a full account.

—Juan de Betanzos, *Cronicas Peruanas de Interes Indigena* (1551)

Dividing the Sexes

One of the most startling things Native Americans and Europeans discovered during their first encounters was their differing ideas about men and women. In most cultures, men and women did, and do, different work but across cultures there is a great deal of variation in the *kinds* of work men and women are expected to do. Social scientists call this the "sexual division of labor." In some Native American societies, women's work was valued highly, and they tended to wield considerable political power. In western Europe, by contrast, women's work was usually confined to activities that were not highly regarded.

English colonists in particular complained at length about how Indian squaws were overworked, and used this perceived distinction between native and European gender systems as yet another marker separating "savagery" from "civilization." In England, hunting was a sport for aristocrats; to New England's colonists, the hunting done by Native American men seemed equally leisurely. In the sexual division of labor among New England's Algonquians men hunted, women farmed, and both contributed to the community's subsistence, an arrangement colonists found appalling. To the Algonquians, English men, who in their eyes did "women's work" in the fields, seemed ridiculously effeminate. In 1634, William Wood offered the following view of Algonquian Indian women's work in New England

for curious readers back in England. In condemning native men as lazy bullies who forced the native women to do all the heavy work, Wood not only depicted the Algonquians as especially backward but also encouraged English women to perceive their lot in life as especially fortunate.

To satisfy the curious eye of women-readers, who otherwise might thinke their sex forgotten, or not worthy a record, let them peruse these few lines, wherein they may see their owne happinesse, if weighed in the womans balance of these ruder *Indians*, who scorne the tuterings of their wives, or to admit them as their equals, though their qualities and industrious deservings may justly claime the preeminence, and command better usage and more conjugall esteeme, their persons and features being every way correspondent, their qualifications more excellent, being more loving, pittifull, and modest, milde, provident, and laborious than their lazie husbands. Their employments be many: First their building of houses. . . . In Winter they make some fiftie or threescore foote long, fortie or fiftie men being inmates under one roofe; and as is their husbands occasion these poor tectionists [house builders] are often troubled like snailes, to carrie their houses on their backs sometimes to fishing-places, other times to hunting-places, after that to a planting place, where it abides the longest: an other work is their planting of corne, wherein they exceede our English husbandmen. . . .

Commendable is their milde carriage and obedience to their husbands, notwithstanding all this their customarie churlishnesse and salvage inhumanitie, not seeming to delight in frownes or offering to word it with their lords, not presuming to proclaime their female superiority to the usurping of the least title of their husbands charter, but rest themselves content under their helplesse condition, counting it the womans portion: since the English arrivall comparison hath made them miserable, for seeing the kind usage of the English to their wives, they doe as much condemne their husbands for unkindnesse, and commend the English for their love.

As writing like Wood's accumulated, an impression began to form among many Europeans that the sexual division of labor among Native Americans was terribly lopsided and that their men were

Iroquois women plant crops (top), collect sap from maple trees (right), and tend to the food preparation for their community. Such scenes convinced Europeans that Indian women were overworked and Indian men were lazy.

essentially freeloaders, an idea that is advanced in the Frenchman Joseph Jouvency's description of Canadian Indians in 1710.

The care of household affairs, and whatever work there may be in the family, are placed upon the women. They build and repair the wigwams, carry water and wood, and prepare the food; their duties and position are those of slaves, laborers and beasts of burden. The pursuits of hunting and war belong to the men. Thence arise the isolation and numerical weakness of the race. For the women, although naturally prolific, cannot, on account of their occupation in these labors, either bring forth fully-developed offspring, or properly nourish them after they have been brought forth; therefore they either suffer abortion, or forsake their newborn children, while engaged in carrying water, procuring wood and other tasks, so that scarcely one infant in thirty survives until youth.

European and Euroamerican misperceptions about men's and women's work in native societies had a great deal of staying power; the stereotype of the "squaw drudge" lasted well beyond the cultures' first encounters, into the 19th century. Like most stereotypes, though, this idea was quickly discarded by those who came to know Indians intimately. One such was Mary Jemison, who was taken captive by the Seneca Iroquois in 1758 and lived among Indians until her death in 1824. (Jemison married a Delaware Indian, with whom she had several children, and refused to rejoin English colonial society.) Here she compares the sexual division of labor in Indian and English colonial communities and finds little discernible difference.

Our labor was not severe. . . . Notwithstanding the Indian women have all the fuel and bread to procure, and the cooking to perform, their task is probably not harder than that of white women, who have those articles provided for them; and their cares certainly are not half as numerous, nor as great. In the summer season, we planted, tended and harvested our corn, and generally had all our children with us; but had no master to oversee us, [presumably because the men were out hunting or warring] so that we could work as leisurely as we pleased. . . . Our cooking consisted in pounding our corn into samp [mush or soup] or hommany [hominy], boiling the hommany, making now and then a cake and baking it in the ashes, and in boiling or roasting our venison.

If Europeans and Native Americans held different beliefs about the proper sexual division of labor, they had perhaps even more divided opinions about men's and women's relative political power and cultural authority. For both peoples, however, those opinions were rooted in "creation stories," descriptions of the origins of the world and the world's peoples (like the Iroquois story about the Turtle's Back in the Introduction). The following creation stories, one a Navajo oral tradition and the other from the written tradition of the Bible, tell us a great deal about Native American and European ideas concerning power and authority.

In the Navajo story, First Man and First Woman find a baby girl who grows up to be the Changing Woman, the mother of all people. Who was created first, man or woman, is undetermined in this story, but clearly Changing Woman is the central, most powerful character.

In the great desert of multicolored sand stood the Mountain-Around-Which-Moving-Was-Done, and at the foot of this great mountain was found a baby girl.

First Man and First Woman found the child when the earth was still unformed and incomplete. They took her home with them and raised her carefully, and the gods smiled on her and loved her. As she grew into womanhood, the world itself reached maturity as the mountains and valleys were all put into the proper places.

At last she was grown and the world was complete, and to celebrate her becoming a woman, the gods gave her a Blessing Way, Walking-into-the-Beauty. . . . But the young girl did not stay the same. Each winter she became withered and white-haired, just as the earth became bare and snow-covered. But each spring as the colors of life grew back on the land, the colors of youth and beauty appeared in her cheeks and in her hair. So she is call[ed] Changing Woman, or "A Woman She Becomes Time and Again."

The sun fell in love with Changing Woman. . . . On the advice of First Woman, she met the sun and he made love to her. Nine months later, twin sons were born to her and she raised them with love and care. For monsters had now appeared in the world, and the people were being destroyed.

[Monsters come and threaten the world, but Changing Woman's twin sons destroy them.]

Now the world was complete and the monsters were dead. It was a perfect place for people, but there were very few left. Changing Woman pondered over this problem, and at last she took baskets of corn. One was of white corn and one was of yellow corn. From the white cornmeal she shaped a man and from the yellow cornmeal she shaped a woman.

And so the earth was populated again, a changing world and a beautiful world—the world of the Changing Woman.

Many Europeans' and Euroamericans' ideas about men and women derived from a very different creation story, in which the first woman is created after the first man and designed to serve him. Nearly all Europeans who came to the New World in the 15th, 16th, and 17th centuries were Christians. Some Europeans, like the French and the Spanish, were Catholic, while others, such as the English and the Dutch, were predominantly Protestant. A small number of Jews also migrated. Nearly all Europeans, however, subscribed to the creation story in Genesis, the first book of the Bible's Old Testament. The Book of Genesis tells how God created first the heavens and the earth and then, over the next five days, created night and day, water and land, animals and plants. On the sixth day God created man, in the form of Adam, and on the seventh day God rested. Only later, because "for Adam there was not found an help meet [partner]," God created Eve, the first woman.

And the Lord God caused a deep sleep to fall upon Adam, and he slept: and he took one of his ribs, and closed up the flesh instead thereof; And the rib, which the Lord God had taken from man, made he a woman, and brought her unto the man. And Adam said, "This is now bone of my bones, and flesh of my flesh: she shall be called Woman, because she was taken out of Man."

Soon after being created, however, Eve was tempted by the serpent to pick fruit from the forbidden tree in the Garden of Eden. For this sin God declared that all of Adam and Eve's descendants were to be punished with the burden of mortality and the stain of the original sin. For Eve, He reserved a special punishment: "Unto the woman [God] said, I will greatly multiply thy sorrow and thy conception; in sorrow thou shalt bring forth children; and thy desire shall be to thy husband, and he shall rule over thee."

A Catalog of Nature

In Genesis, God also gave Adam dominion, or rule, over all the natural world and charged him with the task of naming all the plants and animals. In the New World, which some

Among John White's watercolors of native animals and plants were these images of a land crab, brown pelican, and pineapple.

Europeans took to be a kind of second Eden, Christian Europeans and Euroamericans similarly sought to name and catalog all that they found there. The beauty of this world occasionally left visitors speechless, however. Overwhelmed by the sight of a dramatically plumed bird, a 16th-century Spanish historian, Fernandez de Oviedo lamented, "Of all the things I have seen, this is the one which has most left me without hope of being able to describe it in words." Some early visitors like John White, who made voyages to the coast of Virginia and the Carolinas in the 1580s, tried to describe America's flora and fauna not with words but in pictures. White's watercolors, three of which are shown to the left, depicted many of the plants and animals he saw there. However, many distinctly American plant and animal species became extinct as a result of European diseases and land-use practices.

One German artist and naturalist, Maria Sibylla Merian, traveled to the New World in 1699 specifically to collect and paint the plants, insects, and butterflies to be found there. While living in Amsterdam in the 1690s, Merian had become fascinated with news and drawings of the "marvels of nature" to be found in the newly discovered lands. "I examined with wonder the different kinds of creatures brought back from the East and West Indies," she wrote. Finally, at the age of 52, Merian sailed to the Dutch colony of Suriname, or Surinam, on the north coast of South America, accompanied by her 21-year-old daughter Dorothea. At the time, that country was largely populated by native Arawak Indians and African slaves brought to work the Dutch sugar plantations, and Merian relied on both the Arawaks and the Africans to help her collect and breed native insect and plant species, many of which the local people used as medicines. Merian and her daughter returned to Amsterdam in 1701. Four years later Merian published her *Metamorphosis of the Insects of Suriname*, which earned her an important place in the world of Dutch artists, scientists, botanists, and collectors. The exquisitely detailed plate from the collection shown depicts caterpillars metamorphosing (changing) into moths on a tree in Suriname.

While artists like White and Merian studied and admired the beauty of American plant and animal species, many more Europeans marveled at the fertility and abundance to be found in the New World. European writers described the flora and fauna of the New World in great detail, depicting it as a utopia, a promised land of vast bounty and beauty. For many Europeans, the New World seemed an idyllic setting, a Garden of Eden full of magical places—the fountain of youth, rivers of gold, and enchanted forests.

In 1628, John Leverett, a Massachusetts colonist, tried to dispel some of the myths about New England that earlier writers had made popular in England.

I will not tell you that you may smell the corn fields before you see the land; neither must men think that corn doth grow naturally, (or on trees), nor will the deer come when they are called, or stand still and look on a man until he shoot him, not knowing a man from a beast; nor the fish leap into the kettle, nor on the dry land, neither are they so plentiful, that you may dip them up in baskets, nor take cod in nets to make a voyage, which is no truer than that the fowls will present themselves to you with spits through them.

Indians Abroad

Europeans commonly brought specimens of New World plants and animals to Europe and, from the earliest voyages, were likely to return with Indians as well—by kidnapping, tricking, or persuading them to board their ships. When Maria Sibylla Merian left Suriname for Amsterdam in 1701, she brought back not only bottles of baby crocodiles and snakes, lizards' eggs, flower bulbs, seed packages, and boxes of pressed insects, but also an Indian woman slave. And on Columbus's first voyage he kidnapped nine Taínos and took them to Spain to present them to the royal court. Many of these unfortunate men, women, and children died during the Atlantic voyage or soon after arriving in Europe, but others survived to become proficient translators, interpreters, and ambassadors. While in Europe, Native Americans were often paraded in public to satisfy the popular curiosity, where they drew huge crowds, and they were commonly presented at court.

Giovanni da Verrazano described how he kidnapped several Indians on a voyage in 1523–24 to bring them to France.

After fifty leagues we reached another land which seemed much more beautiful and full of great forests. We anchored there, and with XX men we penetrated about two leagues inland, to find that the people had fled in terror to the forests. Searching everywhere, we met with a very old woman and a young girl of XVIII to XX

A plate from Maria Sibylla Merian's Metamorphosis of the Insects of Suriname *shows a caterpillar and moth on a palisade tree.*

years, who had hidden in the grass in fear. The old woman had two little girls whom she carried on her shoulders, and clinging to her neck a boy—they were all about eight years old. The young woman also had three children, but all girls. When we met them, they began to shout. The old woman made signs to us that the men had fled to the wood. We gave her some of our food to eat, which she accepted with great pleasure; the young woman refused everything and threw it angrily to the ground. We took the boy from the old woman to carry back to France, and we wanted to take the young woman, who was very beautiful and tall, but it was impossible to take her to the sea because of the loud cries she uttered.

In 1509, a French ship returning from Newfoundland brought seven Indians to Rouen, where they gave a demonstration of their boating and fishing skills before a large audience. Six soon died, exposed to Old World diseases.

Seven savage men have been brought from that land, which is called Terre-Neuve [New World], along with their boat, their clothing and their arms. They are the color of soot, have very large lips, and have some tattooing, like a little blueish vein, on the face, running from the eyes to the middle of the chin and across the jaw. Their hair is black and thick like a horse's mane. During the whole of their life they never have any beard or any other hairy growth on their bodies except for the head and the eye-brows. They wear a girdle in which is a little pouch to cover their private parts. They form their words with their lips. Their boat is made from the bark of a tree. With a single hand a man can put it on his shoulders. Their arms are long-bows, with strings made from the gut or sinew of an animal. Their arrows are reeds, tipped with a stone or fishbone. Their food is broiled meat, they drink water. They do not use bread, wine or money. They go about naked or clothed in the skins of animals such as bear, deer, seal and the like. Their land is. . . somewhat below that of France.

Native Americans who were brought to Europe to be exhibited before curious onlookers were no doubt humiliated by the experience, but

In 1625 the English philosopher Francis Bacon recommended that Indians be brought to Europe in order that they might be inspired to imitate it: "Send oft of them over to the country that plants, that they may see a better condition than their own, and commend it when they return." But Native Americans visiting Europe were usually valued not for their conformity to European ways but for their supposed "savagery," which they were encouraged to demonstrate before huge crowds. This poster from 1818 advertises one such event, in Leeds, England.

BY PERMISSION
Of the Worshipful the Mayor of Leeds.

WILD INDIAN
Savages,

From the Borders of Lake Erie,

In the Western Wilds of North-America, who arrived at Liverpool in the Brig Sally, on the 31st Day of January, 1818; THE

Chief & Six Warriors,

Of the Senaca Nation, will continue to exhibit their interesting Performances,

At the Concert-Room, in Albion-Street,

This PRESENT MONDAY EVENING, APRIL 20th, 1818,

And every Evening during the present Week:

And at the particular Request of Ladies and Gentlemen presiding over Seminaries, there will be a

Day Exhibition on Tuesday and Saturday, in the present Week,

Doors to be opened at One and to commence precisely at Two o'Clock.

Monday Evening, April 27th,
WILL POSITIVELY BE THE

LAST NIGHT.

THE PERFORMANCES WILL CONSIST OF A FAITHFUL AND
Correct Representation of their Native Manners and Customs.
For Particulars see Hand-Bills.

EDWARD BAINES, PRINTER, LEEDS.

they probably soon grew keenly aware of just what European crowds expected. Here a Micmac Indian tells the story of Silmoodawa, another Micmac, who made a mockery of the European audience that assembled to watch him the way people watch animals in zoos.

An Indian named Silmoodawa was taken to Planchean [France] as a curiosity. Among other curious adventures, he was prevailed upon to exhibit the Indian mode of killing and curing game. A fat ox or deer was brought out of a beautiful park and handed over to the Indian; he was provided with all the necessary implements, and placed within an enclosure of ropes, through which no person was allowed to pass, but around which multitudes were gathered to witness the butchering operations of the savage.

He shot the animal with a bow, bled him, skinned and dressed him, sliced up the meat, and spread it out on flakes to dry; he then cooked a portion and ate it, and in order to exhibit the whole process, and to take a mischievous revenge upon them for making an exhibition of him, he went into a corner of the yard and eased himself before them all.

First encounters between Europeans and Native Americans were tremendously varied. European peoples had much in common with one another, and many Indian cultures that spread across the continent shared similar traits. There were also tremendous differences, however, between a Sioux Indian and a Delaware Indian, for example, or between a Dutchman and an Englishwoman. Moreover, each culture responded differently to the challenges of meeting new people. A Frenchwoman raised in Paris might have felt differently about an Iroquois child than a Frenchwoman raised in the countryside. Still, the broad patterns suggested here—of excitement and amazement on the one hand, and dismay and even disgust on the other—hint at the outcome of future encounters.

"They will not give a doit [an insignificant coin] to relieve a lame beggar, but they will lay out ten to see a dead Indian."
—William Shakespeare,
The Tempest

Chapter Three

Conquest and Resistance

Get map. [handwritten marginalia]

In 1519, a young girl saw her world change forever, and she helped change it. Malinalli, as she was called, had been living in the town of Tabasco in southeastern Mexico, but in 1519 she left home to accompany a group of Spanish soldiers marching to Tenochtitlán, the heart of the Aztec empire. Malinalli soon became the Spanish expedition's most valuable interpreter. As Aztec messengers sent to observe the Spaniards' progress reported, "The strangers are accompanied by a woman from this land, who speaks our Nahuatl tongue." Before the Spanish arrived in Mexico, Malinalli already had learned to speak two languages: Nahuatl, the language spoken in the Aztec village where she was born, and Mayan, spoken by the people of Tabasco. She quickly learned Spanish, too, so that en route to Tenochtitlán she became indispensable to Hernán Cortés, the leader of the Spanish expedition. As one of Cortés's soldiers observed, "Cortés could not understand the Indians without her." The Aztecs came to call Malinalli La Malinche, adding the suffix -che to her name as a sign of respect, and even to call Cortés El Malinche, since he was always in Malinalli's presence. The Spaniards called her simply Doña Marina.

Malinalli's service to Cortés as a translator contributed to one of the earliest and most brutal invasions in the age of encounters, the Spanish conquest of Tenochtitlán and the Aztec empire. For that reason, many Mexicans and Mexican Americans today revile Malinalli as a traitor to her people. But who were her people? Malinalli was born between 1502 and 1505, the daughter of a village chief within the Aztec empire. Her father died and her mother remarried, then had a son by her new husband. Since Malinalli would have threatened this new son's inheritance, her mother and stepfather sold her into slavery. Then, when the Spanish arrived in Tabasco, the villagers presented Malinalli and nineteen other enslaved women as a gift to Cortés. Did she serve Cortés as a slave, and accompany him only through force? Many Spanish conquistadores raped Indian women, or had consensu-

In this 1598 engraving, Spaniards receive gifts from the Indians. Exchanges of gifts led rapidly into regular trade, and as a result, Native Americans became increasingly dependent on the goods brought by whites. The Spaniards, in turn, wanted increasing amounts of gold to fill their coffers.

[handwritten marginalia: *Was she a traitor?*]

[handwritten marginalia: *How and why is Malinal- La Malinche viewed differently historically? What key role did she play in conquest*]

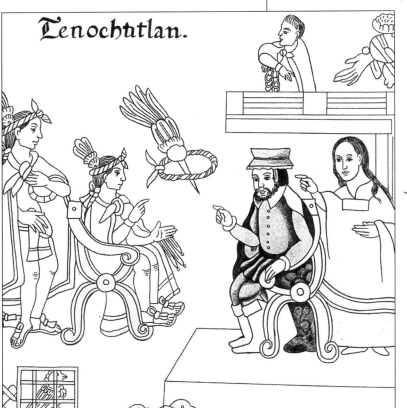

La Malinche (far right) translates for both Cortés (seated, with hat) and the Aztecs (left). By gathering information in this way, Cortés was able to devise a successful strategy for defeating the Indians.

There and then Cortés took possession of that land for His Majesty, performing the act in His Majesty's name. It was done in this way; he drew his sword and as a sign of possession he made three cuts in a huge tree called a Ceiba [silk-cotton tree], which stood in the court of that great square, and cried that if any person should raise objection, that he would defend the right with the sword and shield which he held in his hands.

—Bernal Díaz del Castillo, a member of the Cortés expedition.

al sexual relations with them, and Cortés was no exception. In any case, whether by force or otherwise, Cortés took Malinalli as his mistress and she bore him a son. Later she became the wife of another Spanish soldier. It is thus difficult to say just who Malinalli's people were, and to decide whether she was true to them.

Malinalli spoke three languages because she lived among three peoples. Like many Indians who became translators and interpreters, she lived in the space between cultures. In the age of encounters, living between cultures was a perilous position for anyone, and it must have been all the more treacherous for a woman and a slave. In aiding the Spanish, Malinalli was probably attempting to find a way to survive.

Malinalli met Cortés almost 30 years after Columbus first sailed west, but Spain began its colonizing efforts in the New World almost as soon as Columbus returned home. Over the next three centuries, Spain's North American territories would cross the continent and range as far as Virginia in the east and Canada in the north, covering at least half the continental United States. From the start, Spanish soldiers and settlers were motivated by a search for wealth and a fervent mission to convert the Native Americans to Christianity. As one conquistador put it, "We came here to serve God, and also to get rich."

These two goals were often in tension with one another, however. The riches to be found in New Spain proved abundant—between 1503 and 1520 alone, Spanish ships carried 14,000 kilograms of gold (more than fifteen tons) to Seville. To acquire such riches—which had to be dug from mines, melted down, and purified—the conquistadores forcibly enslaved thousands of Native Americans, which did little to incline the Indians to favor the Europeans' religion. The Spaniards' enslavement and harsh treatment of the Indians they encountered not only hampered the missionary efforts of Spain's Dominican, Franciscan, and Jesuit priests, but gained Spain a reputation as the most oppressive colonial power in the Americas. These tales of Spanish cruelty were later referred to as "black legends" by other European powers seeking to defend their own treatment of the Native Americans.

Malinalli ended up aiding the Spanish and ultimately marrying one of them, but different native peoples who encountered Spanish soldiers, priests, and settlers responded to the foreigners in different ways. When Spanish soldiers arrived at an Indian settlement (most often to plunder it), the residents might greet them with gifts and feasts—or they might meet them with a shower of stones and arrows. During the earliest encounters, many Indian groups, trying to make sense of the strangers, relied on religious traditions and prophecies. Some may have briefly considered the possibility that the Spanish were gods whose arrival had long been predicted. The Aztec leader Montezuma may have believed that Cortés was the god Quetzalcoatl returning to lead his people into an era of peace. However, if the Indians were quick to believe that the Spanish were gods, they were just as quickly disillusioned. Hernando de Soto told the Indians he met in the Southeast in 1539 that he was "a son of the sun," only to be challenged to prove his divinity by drying up the Mississippi River! And, just as some Indians interpreted the Spaniards' arrival as prophetic, many Spaniards were themselves driven by prophecies that led them to search for mythical places like the Fountain of Youth, El Dorado, and the fabled Seven Cities of Cibola.

As word of the Spaniards' mortality and brutality spread, they met with greater and greater native resistance. Meanwhile, along with the arrival of the Spanish, a host of European diseases spread among the native populations. Smallpox especially all but wiped out entire Indian peoples and cultures. As a result, decimated by disease and devastated by the unraveling of their social structure, some native peoples became more receptive to life within Spanish missions, where they attempted to build new kinds of communities.

Montezuma, Quetzalcoatl, and Cortés

The Aztec people of what is now Mexico ruled over a vast territory, exacting tribute from the surrounding peoples called the Toltecs, whom they had conquered in the 13th century. The center of the Aztec empire was the great city Tenochtitlán (on the site of Mexico City), founded in 1325, where, at the time the Spanish arrived, a leader named Montezuma ruled. Aztec accounts written after the Spanish victory over

When they arrived at the treasure house called Teucalco, the riches of gold and feathers were brought out to them: ornaments made of quetzal feathers, richly worked shields, disks of gold, the necklaces of the idols, gold nose plugs, gold greaves [lower-leg armor] and bracelets and crowns.

The Spaniards immediately stripped the feathers from the gold shields and ensigns. They gathered all the gold into a great mound and set fire to everything else, regardless of its value. Then they melted down the gold into ingots. . . . The Spaniards searched through the whole treasure house, questioning and quarreling, and seized every object they thought was beautiful."

—An Aztec description of Spanish greed

What did Montezume, Emperor of the Aztecs believe when he heard report of Cortes and his party's arrival at Mexico?

Quetzalcoatl, the Aztec god of wisdom, is shown in this codex illustration with a conical hat, bird-beaked mask, and shield with feathers. Montezuma believed that Cortés was the long-departed Quetzalcoatl, who had finally returned home.

What does Visual clarity described on pg. 62 revealed about what Aztecs initially thought about Cortes' arrival.

Tenochtitlán claim that in 1519, when Montezuma heard of the arrival of Spanish ships along the coast, he believed that an ancient Toltec prophecy had come to pass: Quetzalcoatl, the god of wisdom who had departed long ago, promising to return by sea, had finally done so. According to one Aztec codex, or manuscript, Montezuma sent messengers carrying gifts to greet Cortés.

When [the messengers] came up to the ships, the strangers asked them: "Who are you? Where are you from?"

"We have come from the City of Mexico."

The strangers said: "You may have come from there, or you may not have. Perhaps you are only inventing it. Perhaps you are mocking us." But their hearts were convinced; they were satisfied in their hearts. They lowered a hook from the bow of the ship, then a ladder, and the messengers came aboard.

One by one they did reverence to Cortés by touching the ground before him with their lips. They said to him: "If the god will deign to hear us, your deputy Montezuma has sent us to render you homage. He has the City of Mexico in his care. He says: 'The god is weary.'"

Then they arrayed the Captain in the finery they had brought him as presents. With great care they fastened the turquoise mask in place, the mask of the god with its crossband of quetzal feathers. A golden earring hung down on either side of this mask. . . .

Next they fastened [a] mirror to his hips, [and] dressed him in the cloak known as "the ringing bell." . . . In his hand they placed [a] shield with its fringe and pendant of quetzal feathers, its ornaments of gold and mother-of-pearl. Finally they set before him [a] pair of black sandals. As for the objects of divine finery, they only laid them out for him to see.

The Captain asked them: "And is this all? Is this your gift of welcome? Is this how you greet people?"

They replied: "This is all, our lord. This is what we have brought you."

The meeting between Cortés and Montezuma, during which Malinalli served as translator, is one of the most dramatic moments in the history of first encounters between the peoples of Europe and the Americas. Because it was recorded by both Cortés and the Aztecs, it offers a rare opportunity to view a meeting from both sides. However, since both of these accounts were written well after the fact, it is wise to be skeptical. The Aztec historians who described this scene were no doubt influenced by the knowledge of what followed—the death of Montezuma and the destruction of Tenochtitlán—while Cortés was writing to impress his sovereign, the king of Spain.

First the Aztec account:

The Spaniards arrived . . . near the entrance to Tenochtitlán. That was the end of the march, for they had reached their goal. Montezuma now arrayed himself in his finery, preparing to go out to

After greeting Montezuma's messengers, Cortés and his soldiers marched inland, toward Tenochtitlán. Along the way they stopped at cities such as Tlaxcala. In this map of Tlaxcala, the Atzompa River bisects the city from north (left) to south. The people of Tlaxcala told Cortés that they were very hated enemies of Montezuma, and they wished to be his allies. As Bernal Diaz del Castillo, one of Cortés's soldiers, later reported, "Cortés found out that Montezuma had opponents and enemies, which he was delighted to hear."

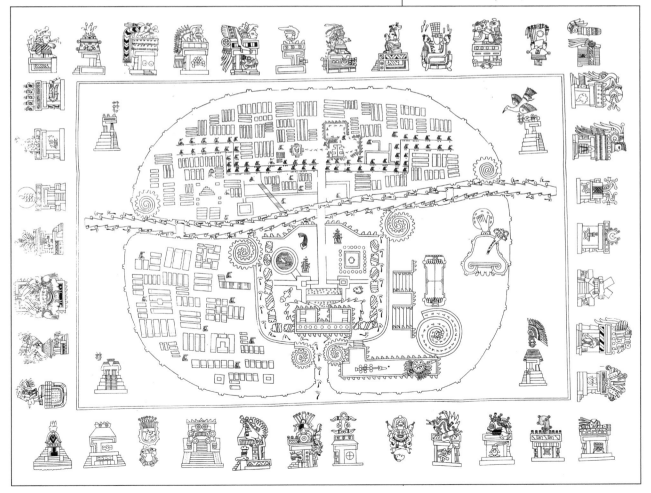

Flowers

Necklaces of gold

Still thinks in Quetz

meet them. The other great princes also adorned their persons, as did the nobles and their chieftains and knights. They all went out together to meet the strangers.

They brought trays heaped with the finest flowers—the flower that resembles a shield; the flower shaped like a heart; in the center, the flower with the sweetest aroma; and the fragrant yellow flower, the most precious of all. They also brought garlands of flowers, ornaments for the breast, necklaces of gold, and necklaces hung with rich stones.

Thus Montezuma went out to meet them. . . . He presented many gifts to the Captain and his commanders, those who had come to make war. He showered gifts upon them and hung flowers around their necks; he gave them necklaces of flowers and bands of flowers to adorn their breasts; he set garlands of flowers upon their heads. Then he hung gold necklaces around their necks and gave them presents of every sort as gifts of welcome.

When Montezuma had given necklaces to each one, Cortés asked him: "Are you Montezuma? Are you the king? Is it true that you are the king Montezuma?"

And the king said: "Yes, I am Montezuma." Then he stood up to welcome Cortés; he came forward, bowed his head low and addressed him in these words: "Our lord, you are weary. The journey has tired you, but now you have arrived on the earth. You have come to your city, Mexico. You have come here to sit on your throne, to sit under its canopy.

"The kings who have gone before, your representatives, guarded it and preserved it for your coming. . . . The people were protected by their swords and sheltered by their shields.

"Do the kings know the destiny of those they left behind, their posterity? If only they are watching! If only they can see what I see!

"No, it is not a dream. I am not walking in my sleep. I am not seeing you in my dreams. . . . I have seen you at last! I have met you face to face! I was in agony for five days, for ten days, with my eyes fixed on the Region of the Mystery. And now you have come out of the clouds and mists to sit on your throne again.

"This was foretold by the kings who governed your city, and now it has taken place. You have come back to us; you have come down from the sky. Rest now, and take possession of your royal houses. Welcome to your land, my lords!"

When Montezuma had finished, La Malinche translated his address into Spanish so that the Captain could understand it. Cortés replied in his strange and savage tongue, speaking first to La Malinche: "Tell Montezuma that we are his friends. There is nothing to fear. We have wanted to see him for a long time, and now we have seen his face and heard his words. Tell him that we love him well and that our hearts are contented."

Then he said to Montezuma: "We have come to your house in Mexico as friends. There is nothing to fear."

La Malinche translated this speech and the Spaniards grasped Montezuma's hands and patted his back to show their affection for him.

This is Cortés's account of the same meeting, from a letter he later wrote to King Carlos V:

There are only two gates, one for entering and one for leaving. Here as many as a thousand men came out to see and speak with me, important persons from that city, all dressed very richly after their own fashion. When they reached me, each one performed a ceremony which they practice among themselves; each placed his hand on the ground and kissed it. And so I stood there waiting for nearly an hour until everyone had performed his ceremony. Close to the city there is a wooden bridge ten paces wide. . . .

After we had crossed this bridge, Montezuma came to greet us and with him some two hundred lords, all barefoot and dressed in a different costume, but also very rich in their way and more so than the others. They came in two columns, pressed very close to the walls of the street, which is very wide and beautiful and so straight that you can see from one end to the other. It is two-thirds of a league long and has on both sides very good and big houses, both dwellings and temples.

Montezuma came down the middle of this street with two chiefs, one on his right hand and the other on his left. One of these was that great chief who had come on a litter to speak with me, and the other was Montezuma's brother. . . . And they were all dressed alike except that Montezuma wore sandals whereas the others went barefoot; and they held his arm on either side. When we met I dismounted and stepped forward to embrace him, but the two lords who were with him stopped me with their hands so that I should not touch him; and they likewise all performed the ceremony of kissing the earth.

When this was over Montezuma requested his brother to remain with me and to take me by the arm while he went a little way ahead with the other; and after he had spoken to me all the others in the two columns came and spoke with me, one after another, and then each returned to his column.

In planning their cities, the Aztecs were influenced by the earlier Toltecs, who incorporated large pyramids with temples into their designs. Wide boulevards and large houses were also characteristic.

When at last I came to speak to Montezuma himself I took off a necklace of pearls and cut glass that I was wearing and placed it round his neck; after we had walked a little way up the street a servant of his came with two necklaces, wrapped in a cloth, made from red snails' shells, which they hold in great esteem; and from each necklace hung eight shrimps of refined gold almost a span [about nine inches] in length. When they had been brought he turned to me and placed them about my neck, and then continued up the street in the manner already described until we reached a very large and beautiful house which had been well prepared to accommodate us. There he took me by the hand and led me to a great room facing the courtyard through which we entered. And he bade me sit on a very rich throne, which he had had built for him and then left saying that I should wait for him. After a short while, when all those of my company had been quartered, he returned with many and various treasures of gold and silver and featherwork, and as many as five or six thousand cotton garments, all very rich and woven and embroidered in various ways. And after he had given me these things he sat on another throne which they placed there next to the one on which I was sitting, and addressed me in the following way:

"For a long time we have known from the writings of our ancestors that neither I, nor any of those who dwell in this land, are natives of it, but foreigners who came from very distant parts; and likewise we know that a chieftain, of whom they were all vassals, brought our people to this region. And he returned to his native land and after many years came again, by which time all those who had remained were married to native women and had built villages and raised children. And when he wished to lead them away again they would not go nor even admit him as their chief; and so he departed. And we have always held that those who descended from him would come and conquer this land and take us as their vassals. So because of the place from which you claim to come, namely, from where the sun rises, and the things you tell us of the great lord or king who sent you here, we believe and are certain that he is our natural lord, especially as you say that he has known of us for some time. So be assured that we shall obey you and hold you as our lord in place of that great sovereign of whom you speak. . . ."

After being lavishly greeted by Montezuma, Cortés neverthe-less took him prisoner. And, while the residents of Tenochtitlán were celebrating the feast of Toxcatl, an important holy day, Spanish soldiers entered the temple and massacred the celebrants. Outraged by the massacre and the many other abuses they had suffered at the hands of the Spanish, the people of Tenochtitlán revolted and forced the Spanish to flee the city. During the confusion Montezuma, who was consid-ered by some of his people to have acted treacherously in welcoming Cortés into the city, was himself killed.

**   After the Spaniards retreated from Tenochtitlán, they gathered up all the Aztecs' enemies to prepare for a renewed attack on the city. Meanwhile, as described in this Aztec codex, a virulent smallpox epidemic broke out in Tenochtitlán, with the result that when the Spanish returned with reinforcements they were able to conquer the weakened capital.**

While the Spaniards were in Tlaxcala, a great plague broke out here in Tenochtitlán. It began to spread during the thirteenth month and lasted for seventy days, striking everywhere in the city and killing a vast number of our people. Sores erupted on our faces, our breasts, our bellies; we were covered with agonizing sores from head to foot.

    The illness was so dreadful that no one could walk or move. The sick were so utterly helpless that they could only lie on their beds like corpses, unable to move their limbs or even their heads. They could not lie face down or roll from one side to the other. If they did move their bodies, they screamed with pain.

After receiving a lavish welcome into Tenochtitlán, Spanish soldiers enter a temple and proceed to massacre the unarmed Aztecs.

Broken spears lie in the roads
we have torn our hair in our grief.
The houses are roofless now,
*   and their walls*
are red with blood.

    —Aztec poem describing the
    destruction of Tenochtitlán

A great many died from this plague, and many others died of hunger. They could not get up to search for food, and everyone else was too sick to care for them, so they starved to death in their beds.

An Eight-Year Journey

Cortés was but one among many early Spanish adventurers attempting to find riches by traveling into the interior of the Americas. Another, Alvar Núñez Cabeza de Vaca, had the misfortune to sign on to an ill-fated expedition headed by Pánfilo de Narváez to explore Florida. In June 1527, Narváez and 600 men left Spain in five ships. After stays in the Caribbean, where part of the crew died in fierce hurricanes, they sailed to Florida, arriving in April 1528. Narváez, Cabeza de Vaca, and some 300 men were left on shore to found a colony, expecting to rendezvous with ships farther along the coast. But the colony failed, and Narváez's ships sailed back to Spain without him. Of the 300 men left in Florida, only four—Cabeza de Vaca, Andrés Dorantes de Carranca, Alonza del Castillo Maldonado, and an African called only Estevánico, or Esteban—survived. After sailing on makeshift boats, headed for Cuba, they landed in Texas, and walked together from Texas to Mexico City, a journey of 600 miles. Eight years later, after enduring long periods of enslavement by the Indians and longer periods of travel, the four finally arrived in Spanish territory. Cabeza de Vaca returned to Spain and wrote a narrative of his experiences, *La Relación que Dió Alvar Núñez Cabeza de Vaca*, that was first published in 1542. In the following passages, he describes how he and his companions became medicine men, or shamans, among the Indians.

They tried to make us into medicine men, without examining us or asking for credentials, for they cure illnesses by blowing on the sick person, and by blowing and using their hands they cast the illness out of him; and they ordered us to do the same and to be of some use. We laughed at it, saying that it was a joke and that we did not know how to heal, and because of this they withheld our food until we did as they had told us. And seeing our resistance, one Indian told me that I did not know what I was talking about when I said that what he knew would be of no use to me, for stones and other things that grow in the fields have virtue, and

The decorative title page from the first edition of Cabeza de Vaca's La Relación que Dió Alvar Núñez Cabeza de Vaca *displays a two-headed crowned bird behind a Spanish coat of arms.*

by using a hot stone and passing it over the stomach he could cure and take away pain; and we, who were superior men, surely had even greater virtue and power. At last we were under such pressure that we had to do it, without fear that we would be held up to scorn for it. The manner they have of curing is as follows: When they find that they are ill they call for a doctor, and after they are cured they not only give him everything they possess but search among their kinfolk for things to give him.

What the doctor does is make some cuts in the place where the patient has the pain and suck all around them. They perform cautery by fire, a thing that is held among them to be very beneficial, and I have tried this and had good results with it; and then they blow on the place where the pain is, and with this they believe that the illness is cured. The way in which we cured was by making the sign of the cross over them and blowing on them and reciting a Pater Noster and an Ave Maria; and then we prayed as best we could to God Our Lord to give them health and inspire them to give us good treatment. God Our Lord, and His mercy, willed that as soon as we made the sign of the cross over them, all those for whom we prayed told the others that they were well and healthy; and because of this they gave us good treatment and went without food themselves in order to give it to us and gave us hides and other small things. . . .

And as throughout the land the people spoke of nothing but the mysteries that God Our Lord had performed through us, they came from many places to find us and have us cure them.

When Cabeza de Vaca finally encountered a Spanish settlement, he attempted to tell the large number of Indians with whom he had been traveling that he must leave them now, but they protested. The nature of their argument—that Cabeza de Vaca could not possibly be a Spaniard because he was a healer, not a killer—reveals a great deal about native perceptions of the Spanish Christians.

They wanted nothing but to go with us until they had left us with other Indians, as their custom was, for if they returned without doing this they were afraid that they would die, and because they were with us they feared neither the Christians [i.e., the Spanish] nor their lances. The Christians were angry at this, and had their interpreter tell them that we were men of their race and that we had been lost for a long time, that we were unlucky and cowardly people, and that they were the masters of that land, whom the

Indians must obey and serve. But the Indians paid little or no heed to what they were told; rather, they talked with one another saying that the Christians were lying, for we came from where the sun rises and they from where it sets; and that we cured the sick and they killed the healthy; and that we had come naked and barefoot and they well dressed and on horses and with lances; and that we did not covet anything, rather we returned everything that they gave us and were left with nothing, and the only aim of the others was to steal everything they found, and they never gave anything to anyone; and so they told all our deeds and praised them, in contrast to the others.

Invading the Interior

Coronado

When Francisco Vásquez de Coronado's expedition arrived at a Zuni pueblo, or village, in present-day New Mexico in 1540, it wasn't unexpected. Scouts from the village had been following the expedition's movements so that, by the time the Spanish arrived, the women, children, and elderly had already been sent away to safety. A group of Zunis attempted to ambush Coronado and his men on the outskirts of town and, as the expedition approached, Zuni warriors "made lines on the earth that no one should pass." The lines, made out of sacred cornmeal, were intended to appeal to the power of the spirits. But the Zunis were willing to appeal to other powers, too, to keep the Spanish out. Just a year before, they had killed Estevánico, or Esteban (the sole African among the four survivors from Narváez's Florida expedition who had made the trek across Texas and Mexico with Cabeza de Vaca) when he approached their town on another expedition. This time, as Coronado's men approached, the Zunis met them with arrows and stones and, when it became clear that they were outnumbered and overpowered, they fled. The Zunis and other Pueblo Indians were soon to be enslaved by the Spanish. As a Zuni tradition relates, "They wore coats of iron, and warbonnets of metal, and carried for weapons short canes that spit fire and made thunder. . . . These black, curl-bearded people drove our ancients about like slave creatures."

In a letter written in August 1540, Coronado described the scene of his first encounter with the Zunis and his surprise at their powerful resistance. He may have been mystified by the Zunis' final act of resistance—abandoning their

They declare that it was foretold them more than fifty years ago that a people such as we are would come, and from the direction we have come, and that the whole country would be conquered.

—Francisco Vásquez de Coronado, on the reaction of the Zuni Indians to the arrival of the Spanish

town—but they had clearly decided that exile was preferable to life under Spanish rule.

As soon as I came within sight of this city, I sent the maestre de campo [aide-de-camp, or assistant] . . . a little way ahead with some horsemen, so that they might find the Indians and tell them that we were not coming to do them any harm, but to defend them in the name of our lord, the emperor. The requisition, in the form which his Majesty commanded in his instructions, was made intelligible to the people of the country through an interpreter. But they, being a proud people, paid little attention to it, because they thought that, since we were few in number, they would have no difficulty in killing us. They pierced the gown of Fray Luis with an arrow, which, blessed be to God, did him no harm.

A Zuni pueblo in New Mexico, photographed in 1879, shows the typical adobe structures that the Indians had built for centuries. Rooms are built one on top of another, with ladders for access.

Meanwhile I arrived with all the rest of the cavalry and footmen and found a large body of Indians on the plain who began to shoot arrows. In obedience to the suggestions of your Lordship and of the marquis, I did not wish that they should be attacked, and enjoined my men, who were begging me for permission, from doing so, telling them that they ought not to molest them, and that the enemy was doing us no harm, and it was not proper to fight such a small number of people. On the other hand, when the Indians saw that we did not move, they took greater courage and grew so bold that they came up almost to the heels of our horses to shoot their arrows. On this account I saw that it was no longer time to hesitate, and, as the priests approved the action, I charged them. There was little to do, because they suddenly took to flight, some running toward the city, which was near and well fortified, and others toward the plain, wherever chance led them. Some Indians were killed, and others might have been slain if I had allowed them to be pursued. But I saw that there would be little advantage in this, because the Indians who were outside were few, and those who had retired to the city, added to the many who had remained there in the first place, were numerous.

As that was the place where the food was, of which we were in such great need, I assembled my whole force and divided it as seemed to me best for the attack on the city, and surrounded it. As the hunger which we suffered would not permit of any delay, I dis-

Before the general arrived, more than two hundred Indian warriors came out, and though they were required to keep the peace, they made lines on the earth that no one should pass, and when our people attempted to do so, they let fly a shower of arrows, and began the attack. Leaving more than twenty dead on the field, they barricaded themselves in their quarters, and later that night they fled.

—A member of Coronado's party, on Zuni resistance to his approach

mounted with several of these gentlemen and soldiers. I ordered the harquebusiers [the harquebus was that day's rough equivalent of today's mortar] and crossbowmen to begin the attack and drive back the enemy from the defenses, so that the natives could not injure us. I investigated the wall on one side, where I was told that there was a scaling ladder and that there was also a gate. But the crossbowmen soon broke the strings of their crossbows and the musketeers could do nothing, because they had arrived so weak and feeble that they could scarcely stand on their feet.

On this account the people who were on the top for defense were not hindered in the least from doing us whatever injury they were able. As for myself, they knocked me down to the ground twice with countless great stones which they threw from above, and if I had not been protected by the very good headpiece which I wore, I think that the outcome would have been bad for me. . . . But, by the pleasure of God, these Indians surrendered, and their city was taken with the help of our Lord, and a sufficient supply of maize to relieve our needs was found there. . . .

Three days after I captured this city, some of the Indians who lived here came to make peace. They brought me some turquoises and poor blankets, and I welcomed them in his Majesty's name with the kindest words I could say, making them understand the purpose of my coming to this country, which is, in the name of his Majesty and by the command of your Lordship, that they and all others in this province should become Christians and should accept the true God as their Lord and his Majesty as their king and earthly master. After this they returned to their houses, and suddenly, the next day, they packed up their goods and property, their women and children, and fled to the hills, leaving their towns deserted, with only some few remaining in them.

One of the first things Coronado did upon arrival at the Zuni village in 1540 was to order the reading of a document called the requerimiento, or requisition, which explained the Spaniards' intentions. This requerimiento became a prelude to some of the most brutal encounters between Spanish soldiers and Native Americans. Before engaging in battle with the Indians, or attempting to capture a village and enslave its inhabitants, the conquistadores were required to read aloud to the Indians a brief statement assuring them that the Spanish had come on a holy mission, blessed by the authority of God through his servant the pope. If the Indians resisted, the requerimiento stated, they would be killed or

[handwritten margin note:] Requerimiento that he read a declaration saying Spanish on a holy mission - if resisted they would be killed or enslaved

enslaved and would have only themselves to blame. In this way, Spain apparently attempted to meet its legal and moral obligations to the inhabitants of the Americas. In many instances, however, the requerimiento was not translated and was read only in Spanish, often at a distance too far away for the Indians to hear. If the Indians could hear and understand the requerimiento, this is what they would have heard:

On the part of the King, don Fernando, and of doña Juana, his daughter, Queen of Castile and León, subduers of the barbarous nations, we their servants notify and make known to you, as best we can, that the Lord our God, Living and Eternal, created the Heaven and the Earth, and one man and one woman, of whom you and I, and all the men of the world, were and are descendants, and all those who come after us. But, on account of the multitude which has sprung from this man and woman in the five thousand years since the world was created, it was necessary that some men should go one way and some another, and that they should be divided into many kingdoms and provinces, for in one alone they could not be sustained.

Of all these nations God our Lord gave charge to one man, called St. Peter, that he should be Lord and Superior of all the men in the world, that all should obey him, and that he should be head of the whole human race, wherever men should live, and under whatever law, sect, or belief they should be; and he gave him the world for his kingdom and jurisdiction. . . .

One of these Pontiffs, who succeeded that St. Peter as Lord of the world . . . made donation of these islands and *terra firme* [continents] to the aforesaid King and Queen and to their successors, our lords, with all that there are in these territories, as is contained in certain writings which passed upon the subject as aforesaid, which you can see if you wish. . . .

Wherefore as best we can, we ask and require you that you consider what we have said to you, and that you take the time that shall be necessary to understand and deliberate on it, and

[handwritten notes in right margin:]
What was the requerimiento and what was its purpose?
What assumptions underlye this document?
That the Pope could claim these lands on the part of the King & Queen of Spain

Pope made donation of these lands to King & Queen of Spain

The Spaniards were brutal in their battles with the Indians and used torture when necessary to subdue or enslave them. Here, one Indian is burned alive while a Spanish priest attempts to convert him and save his soul.

Talking lands for King & Queen & Sam & Pope.

This Governor was much given to the sport of slaying Indians.

—Rodrigo Rangel, on De Soto's throwing Indians to be eaten by dogs

If you do not acknowledge our dominion, we will make war against you and make you slaves

that you acknowledge the Church as the Ruler and Superior of the whole world and the high priest called Pope, and in his name the King and Queen doña Juana, our lords, in his place, as superiors and lords and kings of these islands and this *terra firme.* . . .

If you do so, you will do well, . . . and we in their names shall receive you in all love and charity, and shall leave you your wives, and your children, and your lands free without servitude, . . . and they shall not compel you to turn Christians, unless you yourselves, when informed of the truth, should wish to be converted to our Holy Catholic Faith. . . .

But if you do not do this, and wickedly and intentionally delay to do so, I certify to you that, with the help of God, we shall forcibly enter into your country and shall make war against you in all ways and manners that we can, and shall subject you to the yoke and obedience of the Church and of their Highnesses; we shall take you and your wives and your children, and shall make slaves of them, and as such shall sell and dispose of them as their Highnesses may command; and we shall take away your goods, and shall do all the harm and damage that we can. . . . And that we have said this to you and made this Requirement, we request the notary here present to give us his testimony in writing, and we ask the rest who are present that they should be witnesses of this Requirement.

While Coronado's expedition traveled through the Southwest, another group, led by Hernando de Soto, explored the Southeast. De Soto hoped to repeat his successes in previous expeditions to Central and South America, but he was bitterly disappointed. Instead, he became better known for his extraordinary brutality toward the natives he encountered. The following account, written by his secretary, Rodrigo Rangel, reveals Governor De Soto's manipulation of the dispirited men who accompanied him on his three-year journey through the Southeast.

The Governor had ordered [one of his captains] even though he found no good land, that he should write good news to encourage the men; and, although it was not his nature to lie since he was a man of truth, yet to obey the order of his superior and not to dismay the men, he always wrote two letters of different tenor, one truthful, and the other of falsehoods, yet falsehoods so skillfully framed with equivocal words that they could be understood one way or the other because they required it; and in regard to this, he said that the true letter would have more force to exculpate himself than the false one evil to harm him. And so the Governor did not show the true letters, but announced beforehand that what he did not show was very secret information which later on would be made clear for the great advantage of all. The ambiguous and deceptive letters he showed and made such declarations as seemed best to him.

Those letters, although they promised no particular thing, gave hopes and hints that stirred their desires to go forward and emerge from doubts to certainty; wherefore as the sins of mankind are the reason that falsehood sometimes finds reception and credit, all became united and of one mind and requested the invasion of the land, which was just what the Governor was contriving.

The Great Debate

The cruelties practiced by the Spanish upon the Indians did not go unnoticed in Europe, where Spain's reputation grew into an infamous "black legend." At home, some Spaniards were alarmed by what they heard. In particular, word of widespread torture and enslavement of the Indians so worried the Spanish court that in 1550 King Carlos V summoned a group of theologians, historians, jurists, and philosophers to Valladolid, Spain, to debate the morality and legality of the war against the Indians. While the debate proceeded, Carlos ordered all expeditions to a halt. The great debate at Valladolid centered around whether it was lawful to wage war against the Indians before converting them to Christianity so that, once subjected to Spanish rule, their conversion could be more easily accomplished. At the heart of this issue was the question of whether the Indians were a "civilized" or a "barbarous" people. (Cortés, who did not attend the debate, sent the king a memo expressing his opinion that there ought to be no consideration whatsoever of the Indians' own inclinations: "There is no doubt that the natives must obey the royal orders of Your Majesty, whatever their nature.")

Bartolomé de Las Casas, a Dominican priest, argued that the war against

I have wondered many times at the venturesomeness, stubbornness, and persistency or firmness, to use a better word, for the way those baffled conquerors kept on from one toil to another, and then to another still greater; from one danger to many others, here losing one companion, there three and again still more, going from bad to worse without learning by experience. Oh, wonderful God! that they should have been so blinded and dazed by a greed so uncertain and by such vain discourses as Hernando de Soto was able to utter to those deluded soldiers, whom he brought to a land where he had never been, nor put foot into.

—Rodrigo Rangel, secretary to Hernando de Soto

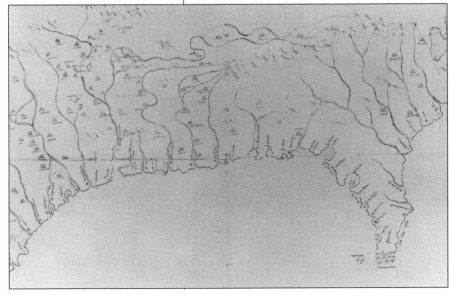

A mid-16th-century map of the Southeast explored by Hernando de Soto provides a rough depiction of Florida at the right. De Soto urged his men for three years to push ahead and invade more Indian territory.

The "Black Legend"

Spain's reputation as an especially cruel colonizing power was fueled by propaganda produced by competing imperial powers. Among the most powerful images of Spanish cruelties are the 16th-century engravings of Theodore de Bry. Yet the exaggerations of the black legend became even more powerful in the 17th century as England, Spain's principal adversary, began its own ventures into North America. In 1656, Las Casas's writings were translated into English, accompanied by gruesome illustrations such as this.

the Indians was unlawful, because the Spanish had an obligation to first attempt to convert the Indians to Christianity before waging war against them. He attempted to discredit scholars who argued that the war was just because the Indians had violated "natural law," standards of behavior that European philosophers believed were intuitively known by all people capable of reason. Among the violations of natural law was cannibalism. At court in Valladolid, Las Casas, who had spent many years preaching to Indians in the New World, argued that the idea that Indians violated natural law was "sheer fables and shameless nonsense."

They who teach, either in word or in writing, that the natives of the New World, whom we commonly call Indians, ought to be conquered and subjugated by war before the gospel is proclaimed and preached to them so that, after they have finally been subjugated, they may be instructed and hear the word of God, make two disgraceful mistakes. First, in connection with divine and human law they abuse God's words and do violence to the Scriptures, to papal decrees, and to the teaching handed down from the holy fathers. And they go wrong again by quoting historians that are nothing but sheer fables and shameless nonsense. By means of these, men who are totally hostile to the poor Indians and who are their utterly deceitful enemies betray them. Second, they mistake the meaning of the decree or bull of the Supreme Pontiff Alexander VI, whose words they corrupt and twist in support of their opinions. . . .

And so what man of sound mind will approve a war against men who are harmless, ignorant, gentle, temperate, unarmed, and destitute of every human defense? For the results of such a war are very surely the loss of the souls of that people who perish without knowing God and without the support of the sacraments, and, for the survivors, hatred and loathing of the Christian religion. Hence the purpose God intends, for the attainment of which he suffered

Las Casas
objects
Didamo 98

[handwritten annotations: We are destroying people before they get to know Christ & we are turning others against us]

so much, may be frustrated by the evil and cruelty that our men wreak on them with inhuman barbarity. What will these people think of Christ, the true God of the Christians, when they see Christians venting their rage against them with so many massacres, so much bloodshed without any just cause, at any rate without any just cause that they know of (nor can one even be imagined), and without any fault committed on their part against the Christians?

Juan Ginés de Sepúlveda, Spain's royal historian, argued against Las Casas and insisted that the war was lawful. Sepúlveda had never traveled to the Americas but, relying on the very scholars Las Casas had discredited, he attempted to argue that the Indians had indeed violated natural law and could thus be justly enslaved.

Authority and power are not only of one kind but of several varieties. . . . And thus we see that among inanimate objects, the more perfect directs and dominates, and the less perfect obeys its command. This principle is even clearer and more obvious among animals, where the mind rules like a mistress and the body submits like a servant. In the same way the rational part of the soul rules and directs the irrational part, which submits and obeys. All of this derives from divine and natural laws, both of which demand the perfect and most powerful rule over the imperfect and the weaker. . . .

The man rules over the woman, the adult over the child, the father over his children. . . . And so it is with the barbarous and inhumane peoples [the Indians] who have no civil life and peaceful customs. It will always be just and in conformity with natural law that such people submit to the rule of more cultured and humane princes and nations. Thanks to their virtues and the practical wisdom of their laws, the latter can destroy barbarism and educate these people to a more humane and virtuous life. And if the latter reject such rule, it can be imposed upon them by force of arms. Such a war will be just according to natural law. . . . Such being the case, you can well understand . . . that with perfect right the Spaniards rule over these barbarians of the New World . . . who in wisdom, intelligence, virtue, and humanitas [humanitarian impulses] are as inferior to the Spaniards as infants to adults and women to men. There is as much difference between them as there is between cruel, wild peoples and the most merciful peoples . . . that is to say, between apes and men. . . .

Bartolomé de Las Casas wrote In Defense of the Indians, *a passionate plea to end the cruelty inflicted upon the Indians.*

[handwritten annotation: force of arms justified]

Engravings, such as this one of Indian cannibals roasting body parts on a fire and pouring molten gold down the throats of Spaniards, were used as propaganda in Europe to either condemn or justify European treatment of the Indians.

How are we to doubt that these people, so uncultivated, so barbarous, and so contaminated with such impiety and lewdness, have not been justly conquered by so excellent, pious, and supremely just a king as Ferdinand the Catholic was and the Emperor Charles [King Carlos, also the Holy Roman Emperor] now is, the kings of a most humane and excellent nation rich in all varieties of virtue?

Missions and Presidios

The debate at Valladolid in 1550 only briefly slowed Spain's colonization of the New World. Over the next two centuries, "New Spain" would grow to encompass lands in Mexico and in much of what is now the continental U. S., bringing incredible wealth to Spain. By the late 18th century, Spain was attempting to secure its foothold on more northern territories by expanding up the Pacific Coast. There, Spain established a chain of missions and presidios, or forts. Jesuit priests had founded missions in Baja [Lower] California, now a part of Mexico, before 1769, when Junípero Serra, a Franciscan, founded a mission in San Diego. Over the next thirteen years, an army of priests and soldiers set up missions in nine sites along the California coast. Four of these missions were accompanied by presidios. As one Franciscan reported to his superior in 1784, "The spiritual conquest had something of the rapid progress that your Excellency wished."

The California missions marshaled enormous wealth for Spain and, later, Mexico. Under the mission system, Franciscan friars attempted to convert the local Indians to Christianity and have them live in a *congregacion*, a congregation or parish, within the confines of the mission. There the mission Indians, called neophytes, labored—often under harsh conditions—to build housing, plant crops, and manufacture goods for the Spanish.

At the time of the Spaniards' arrival, Alta [Upper, or present-day] California was the most densely populated area in North America. However, the spread of European diseases, especially among Indians confined to the small area of the missions, led to a precipitous population decline. In 1769 the Indian population of what is now California was probably about 300,000; by 1821 it was only 200,000. As one Franciscan observed, "They live well free but as soon as we reduce them to a Christian and community life . . . they fatten, sicken, and die."

Junípero Serra documented the history of the Spanish missions in California not only in his own diary, but also in lengthy frequent letters to other missionaries and colonial authorities in Mexico and Spain. After founding the San Diego mission in 1769, Serra traveled up and down the coast of California visiting other missions and issuing reports on the progress of efforts to convert the local Indians to Christianity. The following excerpts, from a series of letters Serra wrote over a four-year period during visits to a single mission at Monterey, illustrate some of the difficulties and obstacles to conversion, as well as the tenacity of native religious beliefs and practices.

A 1541 map of lower California indicates where Spanish missions have been established along the coast.

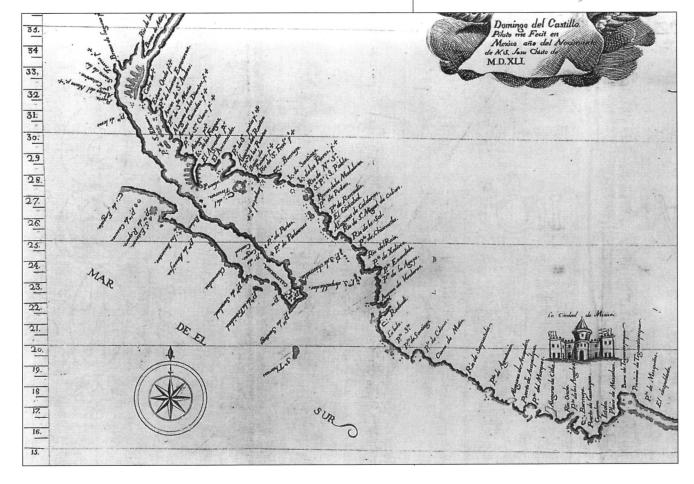

A New Mexican carving of the holy trinity resembles Junípero Serra in all three faces, although the Catholic Church forbade such realistic depictions.

Junípero Serra founded nine missions in California. Under his leadership, thousands of Indians converted to Christianity, and Serra provided them with food and clothing. But he also forced the Indians to live and work at the missions. When Pope John Paul II beatified Serra in 1988, the Cahuilla Indians protested.

[July 2, 1770]
From the Indians who are living a little distance from here I received, today, word by two good Indians I sent them, that they are busy with their harvest; and that four days from now they will come and leave their small children with me. They sent me a little fresh deer meat. May God reward them. I am hoping—*Deo volente* [God willing]—that during the eight days that the boat still has to stay, I will be able to write some more agreeable news to Your Most Illustrious Lordship. Anyway, for the present, suffice it to say that we are here; we will do all we can.

[June 18, 1771]
By God's great mercy, in the short time we have been here, we have already registered twenty Baptisms. Of their number, there are four big boys who not only are able to say their prayers well, but are making much progress in the Castilian tongue; and I, as best I can, am learning from them, as my teachers, the language of this country. At San Diego the number baptized is a little smaller, but the progress of two full-grown boys in the Castilian tongue is greater. These two young Christians serve as interpreters to the gentiles, and as teachers to the Fathers. And so I hope that, by fanning the flame on all sides, by way of these said new missions . . . we will see, before long, new and immense territories gathered into the bosom of our Holy Mother the Church, and subjected to the Crown of Spain.

[June 21, 1771]
The gentiles still continue to be as docile as ever, without any outbreaks. I have administered twenty Baptisms, and if I had known the language, I think I would have baptized them all, with the help of God. Four big boys, Francisco, Buenaventura, Fernando and Diego, are beginning to understand Castilian, but as yet they do not speak it. But we have quite an idea we are going to try out. Two of the boys, Buenaventura and Fernando, one about eight, the other about ten years old, will go with the boat, so attached to it have they become. One will be put in charge of the Captain, the other of the Quartermaster, on the understanding that they are to be returned without fail when the boat comes back. The whole idea is that by the time they return they will both speak Spanish like natives.

[August 8, 1772]
As regards spiritual matters, much could have been accomplished

if only there were something to eat, especially, too, if we could remove some obstacles which I will explain later. . . . What I may say is that, before long, with the help of God, we will have interpreters, and that the gentiles are still, as when we arrived, docile, friendly and peaceful. For many a league the only salutation you hear is: "Love God! Hail Jesus, Mary, Joseph! Holy Cross!" When sighing they say: "Oh Jesus!" And they use other similar expressions.

[August 18, 1772]

All the ministers are groaning—we all feel the weight of the vexations, hardships, and contradictions we have to face; but none of us wishes, or intends to leave his mission. The fact is that, hardships or no hardships, there are many souls sent to heaven from Monterey, San Antonio [de Padua, near Monterey] and San Diego. . . . There are also a goodly number of Christians who give praise to God, whose Holy Name is more frequently in the mouths of these very gentiles than in the mouths of a great many Christians. And even though some claim that these gentle sheep, as they all are, will some day turn into tigers and lions, and it may be so, if God permits it, at any rate, as regards those of Monterey, where we have almost three years of experience, and with those of San Antonio, almost two years, with each passing day they improve. . . . If, at the present time, they are not as yet all Christians, it is, in my judgment, only for want of a knowledge of their language, a trouble of long standing with me which I have never been granted the grace to overcome, it seems to me, because of my many sins. But in countries like these, where it is impossible to get hold of an interpreter, or anybody who can act as an instructor, until someone from t he locality can learn Spanish, it is unavoidable that some time should be required.

Yet, in San Diego, time has overcome the difficulty, and they already have baptized adults in solemn marriages. And here, too, we are not far from arriving at the same state of improvement, since the children are beginning to express themselves in Castilian.

[June 21, 1774]

In this mission alone, where but yesterday there had never been pronounced the name of God nor of Jesus Christ, more than two

The Spanish friars in California attempted to rid the Indians of their native rituals, including dances like this one at the San José mission, in order to prepare them for Christian practices.

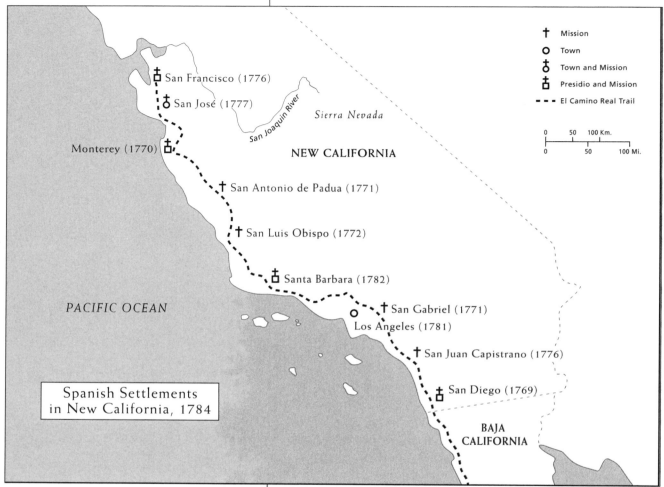

Spanish Settlements
in New California, 1784

*Serra's missionary efforts began
with the founding of the mission
at San Diego in 1769, and moved
northward. Meanwhile, Spain built
a chain of military fortresses, or
presidios, along the coast.*

hundred souls, counting Christians and catechumens. Three times a day they eat from what we provide them; they pray, sing and work; and from the labor of their hands we can boast of fields of wheat, corn, beans, peas, and a garden chock-full of cabbage, lettuce and all kinds of vegetables.

[June 22, 1774]
Father President had taken with him to Mexico from this Monterey Mission an Indian recently baptized. On his return, and when they were nearing his native country, the Father was teaching the Indian how he should explain to the other Indians what he had seen.

And so, he asked him if he or his fellow countrymen, when they saw the officers and soldiers, had ever imagined a country where everybody wore clothes, etc.?

He answered no, that they thought all countries were like their own. As regards the soldiers and the Fathers, after carefully looking them over, they had come to the conclusion that they were the sons of the mules on which they rode.

The Father, in reply, said: "According to that, you must imagine that there are countries where mules give birth to men, and make cotton and cloth?"

"No," he said, "but our old men tell us they come out from under the ground, and that they are—so they say—the souls of old gentiles of the surrounding countries, who have come back this way." But now he knew that all of this was a falsehood, and he would tell the rest so.

After that the Father asked him: "Why is it that when we first came to these parts, and had set up two crosses near Monterey, on our return here, we found that the gentiles had hung on the arms strings of sardines and pieces of deer meat, and at the foot of the cross had shot many broken arrows?"

He answered: "They had done so, that the cross"—porpor was the name they gave it—"might not be angry with them." And to explain why they were afraid, he said that the sorcerers and priest-dancers who roam through the night saw the cross, each night, going up high in the heavens—not of dark material as wood is, but resplendent with light, and beautiful to behold; and for that reason they regarded it with great respect, and made presents to it of all they had.

Pablo Tac, a Luiseño Indian, was born at the Mission of San Luis Rey in southern California in 1822. His description of mission life is the only such account written by an Indian that survives today. Like many mission Indian children, Tac attended the mission school. In 1832, when he was 10 years old, he was chosen to travel first to Mexico and later to Spain and Rome, where he studied for several years at the Vatican. In Rome, Tac worked on a dictionary of his native language, Luiseño, and trained as a missionary. He was never able to return to California but died in Rome in 1841, just before his twentieth birthday. In this account, Tac describes the arrival of the Spanish in California, as well as daily life in the Mission of San Luis Rey.

When the missionary arrived in our country with a small troop, our captain and also the others were astonished, seeing them from afar, but they did not run away or seize arms to kill them, but having sat down, they watched them. But when they drew near, then the captain got up (for he was seated with the others) and met them. They halted, and the missionary then began to speak, the captain saying perhaps in his language "hichsom iva haluon, pulúchajam cham quinai." ["What is it that you seek here? Get out of our country!"] But they did not understand him, and they answered him in Spanish, and the captain began with signs, and the Fernandino Father, understanding him, gave him gifts and in this manner made him his friend. The captain, turning to his people (as I suppose) found the whites all right, and so they let them sleep here. There was not then a stone house, but all were camps (as they say). This was that happy day in which we saw white people, by us called Sosabitom. O merciful God, why didst Thou leave us for many centuries, years, months and days in utter darkness after Thou camest to the world? Blessed be Thou from this day through future centuries.

The Fernandino Father remains in our country with the little troop that he brought. A camp was made, and here he lived for many days. In the morning he said Mass, and then he planned how he would baptize them, where he would put his house, the church, and as there were five thousand souls (who were all the Indians there were), how he could sustain them, and seeing how it could be done. Having the captain for his friend, he was afraid of nothing. It was a great mercy that the Indians did not kill the Spanish when they arrived, and very admirable, because they have never wanted another people to live with them, and until those days they were always fighting. But thus willed He who alone can will. I do not know if he baptized them before making the church or after having made it, but I think he baptized them before making it. He was already a good friend of the captain, and also dear to the neophytes. They could understand him somewhat when he, as their father, ordered them to carry stone from the sea (which is not far) for the foundations, to make bricks, roof tiles, to cut beams, reeds and what was necessary. They did it with the masters who were helping them, and within a few years they finished working. They made a church with three altars for the neophytes (the great altar is nearly all gilded), two chapels, two sacristies, two choirs, a flower garden for the church, a high tower with five bells, two small and three large, the cemetery with a crucifix in the middle for all those who die here. . . .

The Fernandino Father, as he was alone and very accustomed to the usages of the Spanish soldiers, seeing that it would be very difficult for him to give orders to that people, and, moreover, people that had left the woods just a few years before, therefore appointed alcaldes [magistrates] from the people themselves that

The mission at San Luis Rey as it looked around 1840.

knew how to speak Spanish more than the others and were better than the others in their customs. There were seven of these alcaldes, with rods as a symbol that they could judge the others. The captain dressed like the Spanish, always remaining captain, but not ordering his people about as of old, when they were still gentiles. . . .

Returning to the villages, each one of the alcaldes, wherever he goes cries out what the missionary has told them, in his language, and all the country hears it. "Tomorrow the sowing begins and so the laborers go to the chicken yard and assemble there."

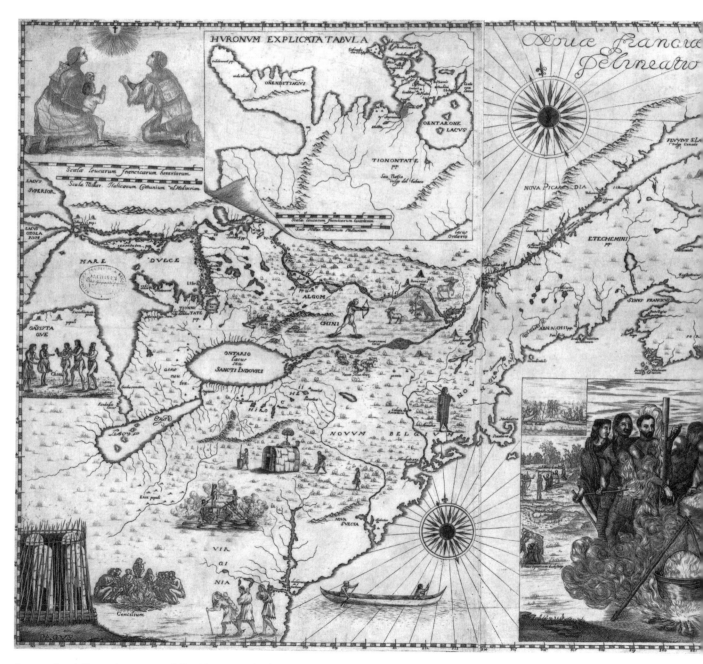

François-Joseph Bressani's 1657 map of New France provides detailed images of Indian activities in the region. Europeans were fascinated with stories of the New World, and Bressani's map serves as a record of Native Americans' daily lives and how they were changing as a result of encounters with the French.

Chapter Four

Furs, Rivers, and Black Robes

I
n 1642, François-Joseph Bressani, a young Jesuit priest, left Rome to embark upon a mission on which he believed he might best serve God. He first traveled westward across the Atlantic, then southward down the St. Lawrence River to Québec, a French outpost that had been founded by Samuel de Champlain in 1608. For a while, Bressani stayed in Québec to preach to French soldiers and traders, but before the year was through he moved on to Three Rivers to try to convert the local Algonquian Indians. Once there, Bressani became restless again and eager to extend his mission to the Indians still more remote from Christian influence. Accordingly, in April 1644, Bressani and several Indian guides set out for the Huron Territory. Along the way, however, they were captured by Mohawks, from whom Bressani endured brutal tortures for two months before finally being ransomed by the Dutch, who had established their own New World colonies in lands farther south, which they called New Netherlands. Although the young Jesuit was able to return to continue his missionary work both at Three Rivers and at the Huron mission, in 1650 his declining health forced him to return to France. There, in 1657, Bressani made a remarkable map of the land that Europeans had come to call New France.

Bressani's story and, even more vividly, his map tell us a great deal about encounters between Europeans and Native Americans in the part of the world we now think of as Canada, the Great Lakes region, northern New England, and upstate New York. A drawing at the bottom right-hand corner of the map illustrates the brutal tortures that Jesuits like Bressani endured at the hands of the Iroquois, while a smaller illustration diagonally opposite, in the upper left-hand corner, shows Christianized Huron Indians piously worshiping a crucifix. The rendering of the map itself emphasizes a crucial fact about New France: the importance of its networks of rivers and lakes that made travel and trade possible. (Below the map's bottom wind-rose, or compass rose, a depiction of Indians paddling in a canoe suggests how well adapted native modes of transportation were to the riverways.) Near the very center of the map, an Indian hunter has been drawn in to signal the importance of the fur trade.

If Bressani's map includes many telling details, it also misses a good bit of the story. We need to look elsewhere to discover, among other things, why the Iroquois took Bressani and other Jesuits captive, why the Hurons converted to Christianity, and why so many Indians engaged in the fur trade. To answer those questions, we need to better understand the Indians Bressani encountered.

The Peoples of the Longhouse

The Mohawks who took François-Joseph Bressani captive were members of a powerful confederacy called the Peoples of the Longhouse. Also known as the Five Nations or the Iroquois League, the Peoples of the Longhouse—Mohawks, Oneidas, Onondagas, Cayugas, and Senecas—had united sometime between 1400 and 1600, when a peacemaker named Daganowedah negotiated the union. The following Iroquois tradition tells the story of how the league was founded and suggests the importance of diplomacy in Iroquois life.

There sprang up among the Onondagas a man more formidable in war than a whole tribe or nation. He consequently became the terror of all the surrounding nations, especially of the Cayugas and Senecas. This man, so formidable and whose cabin was as impregnable as a tower, is said to have had a head of hair, the ends of each terminating in a living snake; the ends of his fingers, and toes, his ears, nose & lips, eye brows & eye lashes all terminated in living snakes. . . .

Among the Onondagas there lived a man [named Daganowedah] renowned for his wisdom, and his great love of peace. For a long time he had watched with great anxiety the increasing power of this military despot who on account of his snakey habiliments, was known by the applicable name Tadodahoh, or Atotahoh, signifying tangled because the snakes seemed to have tangled themselves into his hair. . . . [Daganowedah] concluded to call a general council, of the Five Nations, and to invite to this council the Tadodahoh, at which he proposed to lay before the wise men a plan of Union that would secure not only amity and peace among themselves, and a perpetual existence as a confederacy, but they would render themselves formidable & superior in power to any nation on the Continent.

[Daganowedah proceeded to visit each of the five nations, proposing his plan. He arranged for the Mohawk chief to be his spokesman at a general council.]

To this arrangement the Mohawk agreed. He agreed also to divest Tadodahoh of his snakes, and to make him as other men, except that he should clothe him in civil power as the Head of the Confederacy that should be formed. They then proceeded with a delegation of the Mohawks to the council grounds at Onondaga. When they had arrived they addressed Tadodahoh, the great military despot. The Mohawk divested him of his snakes, and for this reason he was styled Hayowethah, or one who takes away or divests.

The plan of alliance was at first simple. It provided for the establishment of a confederacy, enjoying a democratic form of government. . . . The Union was to be established as a family organization, the Mohawks, Onondagas and Senecas to compose the Fathers and the Cayugas and Oneidas the children. This plan was adopted.

The Peoples of the Longhouse lived in clans named after important animals—Bear, Wolf, and Turtle. Like their other Indian neighbors, the Iroquois believed that animals were sentient beings, like people, and possessed a spiritual force that had to be respected. While the Iroquois relied on killing animals for sustenance, their rituals of hunting and food preparation honored the sacredness of animal life. In the following document, neighbors of the Iroquois, the Cree, explain their traditional beliefs about the beaver and describe how those beliefs changed after the arrival of the Europeans when, as the Iroquois saw it, the Great Spirit became angry with the beaver.

They said, by ancient tradition of which they did not know the origen [sic] the Beavers had been an ancient People, and then lived on the dry land; they were always Beavers, not Men, they were wise and powerful, and neither Man, nor any animal made war on them.

The typical Iroquois longhouse was home to several families who shared fires for cooking and heating.

They were well clothed as at present, and as they made no use of fire, and did not want it. How long they lived this way we cannot tell, but we must suppose that they did not live well, for the Great Spirit became angry with them, and ordered Weesaukejauk [another spirit being] to drive them all into the water and there let them live, still to be wise, but without power; to be food and clothing for man, and the prey of other animals, against all of which his defense shall be his dams, his house and his burrows. . . .

The old Indian paused, became silent, and then in a low tone [the two Cree] talked with each other; after which he continued his discourse. I have told you that we believed in years long passed away, the Great Spirit was angry with the Beaver, and ordered Weesaukejauk . . . to drive them all from the dry land into the water; and they became and continued very numerous; but the Great Spirit has been, and now is, very angry with them and they are now all to be destroyed.

Each had two sticks, which they struck together, and they marched in this order at a slow pace until they arrived at their enclosure. The deer hearing this noise flee before them until they reach the enclosure, into which the savages force them to go. Then they gradually unite on approaching the bay and opening of their triangle, the deer skirting the sides until they reach the end, to which the savages hotly pursue them, with bow and arrow in hand ready to let fly. On reaching the end of the triangle they begin to shout and imitate wolves, which are numerous, and which devour the deer. The deer, hearing this frightful noise, are constrained to enter the retreat by the little opening, whither they are very hotly pursued by arrow shots. Having entered this retreat, which is so well closed and fastened that they can by no possibility get out, they are easily captured.

—Samuel de Champlain (1615)

Like all Native American peoples, the Five Nations that made up the Iroquois League suffered extraordinary losses from disease after their initial contacts with Europeans in the early 16th century. Still more Iroquois died in wars with neighboring Indians and against encroaching French, English, and Dutch settlers. By the time François-Joseph Bressani drew his map of New France in 1657, the disruptions that had upset Native American communities had led the Peoples of the Longhouse to interact with their animal and human neighbors in fundamentally new ways. Now they hunted beaver and other animals not to satisfy basic needs but to participate in a market economy, trading their pelts for European goods like knives, kettles, guns, and alcohol, on which they had become increasingly dependent. One historian has speculated that, since some European diseases affected both animals and humans, Native Americans engaged in the fur trade with great ferocity—ultimately destroying the very animals whose meat had once nourished them and whose spirits had once

guided them—because they blamed these animals for the diseases they suffered in common. In the next extract, a Jesuit missionary reports on how a Montagnais Indian mocked the Europeans' interest in furs. The Montagnais also suggests, however, the degree to which the Native Americans had come to depend on European goods.

"The Beaver does everything perfectly well, it makes kettles, hatchets, swords, knives, bread; and, in short, it makes everything." He was making sport of us Europeans, who have such a fondness for the skin of this animal and who fight to see who will give the most to these Barbarians, to get it; they carry this to such an extent that my host said to me one day, showing me a very beautiful knife, "The English have no sense; they give us twenty knives like this for one Beaver skin."

A New France

In July 1534, Iroquois Indians fishing off the shores of Honguedo (the Gaspé Peninsula) sailed in their canoes to meet a French ship. Donnacona, the leader of the group, greeted Jacques Cartier, the leader of the French expedition. Well before Cartier's arrival, and even before the voyage of Giovanni Verrazano ten years earlier, Indians living near Honguedo had met Europeans, who for many years had fished in these coastal waters. When Cartier arrived in 1534, the French attempted to claim the shore land as their own. They even erected a cross overlooking the harbor, and pointed toward the heavens to explain the cross's significance to the onlooking Indians. Reading between the lines of Cartier's account, it appears that Donnacona was suspicious of Cartier's motives, and rightly so. Cartier soon kidnapped two of Donnacona's sons, Domagaya and Taignoaguy, to guide him on his return voyage. Then, when Cartier returned the next year, he kidnapped Donnacona himself, along with nine other Iroquois, and brought them back to France in 1536, where all ten died. Cartier's description of his meeting with Donnacona and the coastal Iroquois is very hard to evaluate. As with Columbus's logbook and other descriptions of first encounters, it is difficult to know how much to trust Cartier's account. Like Columbus, Cartier is confident that he will be able to communicate with the people he meets, but we know that he had no knowledge of the Iroquois language.

Cartier Visits Hochelaga

During Cartier's second voyage to North America, in 1535, Donnacona's sons, Domagaya and Taignoaguy, guided him to the city of Hochelaga (now Montreal), a Huron settlement on the St. Lawrence River. Here Cartier describes Hochelaga, where he was greeted by more than a thousand Hurons:

In the middle of these fields is situated and stands the village of Hochelaga, near and adjacent to a mountain, the slopes of which are fertile and are cultivated, and from the top of which one can see for a long distance. We named this mountain "Mount Royal." The village is circular and is completely enclosed by a wooden palisade in three tiers like a pyramid. The top one is built crosswise, the middle one perpendicular and the lowest one of the strips of wood placed lengthwise. The whole is well

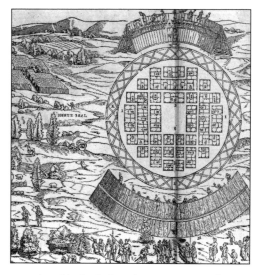

joined and lashed after their manner, and is some two lances in height. There is only one gate and entrance to this village, and that can be barred up. Over this gate and in many places about the enclosure are species of galleries with ladders for mounting to them, which galleries are provided with rocks and stones for the defense and protection of the place. There are some fifty houses in this village, each about fifty or more paces in length, and twelve or fifteen in width, built completely of wood and covered in and bordered up with large pieces of the bark and rind of trees, as broad as a table, which are well and cunningly lashed after their manner. And inside these houses are many rooms and chambers; and in the middle is a large space without a floor, where they light their fire and live together in common.

During that time there arrived a large number of savages, who had come to the river to fish for mackerel, of which there is great abundance. They numbered, as well men, women as children, more than 300 persons, with some forty canoes. When they had mixed with us a little on shore, they came freely in their canoes to the sides of our vessels. We gave them knives, glass beads, combs and other trinkets of small value, at which they showed many signs of joy, lifting up their hands to heaven and singing and dancing in their canoes. This people may well be called savage; for they are the sorriest folk there can be in the world, and the whole lot of them had not anything above the value of five sous, their canoes and fishing-nets excepted. They go quite naked, except for a small skin, with which they cover their privy parts, and for a few old furs which they throw over their shoulders. They are not at all of the same race or language as the first we met. . . . They have no other dwelling but their canoes, which they turn upside down and sleep on the ground underneath. They eat their meat almost raw, only warming it a little on the coals; and the same with their fish. . . .

On the twenty-fourth of the said month, we had a cross made thirty feet high, which was put together in the presence of a number of the Indians on the point at the entrance to this harbor, under the cross-bar of which we fixed a shield with three fleurs-de-lys in relief, and above it a wooden board engraved in large Gothic characters, where was written LONG LIVE THE KING OF FRANCE. We erected this cross on the point in their presence and they watched it being put together and set up. And when it had been raised in the air, we all knelt down with our hands joined, worshipping it before them; and made signs to them, looking up and pointing toward heaven, that by means of this we had our redemption, at which they showed many marks of admiration, at the same time turning and looking at the cross.

When we had returned to our ships, the chief, dressed in an old black bear-skin, arrived in a canoe with three of his sons and his brother; but they did not come so close to the ships as they had usually done. And pointing to the cross he made us a long harangue, making the sign of the cross with two of his fingers; and then he pointed to the land all around about, as if he wished to say that all this region belonged to him, and that we ought not to have set up this cross without his permission. And when he had finished his harangue, we held up an axe to him, pretending we would barter it for his fur-skin. To this he nodded assent and little by little drew near the side of our vessel, thinking he would have the axe. But one of our men, who was in our dinghy, caught hold of his canoe, and at once two or three more stepped down into it and made the Indians come on board our vessel, at which they were greatly astonished. When they had come on board, they were assured by the captain that no harm would befall them, while at the same time every sign of affection was shown to them; and they were made to eat and to drink and to be of good cheer. And then we explained to them by signs that the cross had been set up to serve as a land-mark and guide-post on coming into the harbor, and that we would soon come back and would bring them iron wares and other goods; and that we wished to take two of his sons away with us and afterward would bring them back again to that harbor. And we dressed up his two sons in shirts and ribbons and in red caps, and put a little brass chain round the neck of each, at which they were greatly pleased; and they proceeded to hand over their old rags to those who were going back on shore. To each of these three, whom we sent back, we also gave a hatchet and two knives at which they showed great pleasure. When they had returned on shore, they told the others what had happened. About noon on that day, six canoes came off to the ships, in each of which were five or six Indians, who had come to say goodbye to the two we had detained, and to bring them some fish. These made signs to us that they would not pull down the cross, delivering at the same time several harangues which we did not understand.

In acquiring geographical knowledge, Cartier, like all Europeans, relied on native informants. As he wrote, "They . . . explained to us by signs that after passing the rapids, one could navigate along that river for more than three moons. And they showed us furthermore that along the mountains to the north, there is a large river, which comes from the west like the said river."

In 1608, Samuel de Champlain established the first permanent French outpost in North America, a tiny settlement called Québec, located at the site of the former Iroquois town of Stadacona, whose residents had abandoned it after an epidemic arrived. The next year, after establishing the settlement, Champlain and a party of Frenchmen set out on expeditions to neighboring communities, attempting to secure allies against the Iroquois and to develop trading partnerships. The Algonquian peoples living in territory that would later be called New France quickly allied themselves with the French, in the hopes of keeping the Iroquois, their long-standing enemies, at bay. When a group of Algonquians

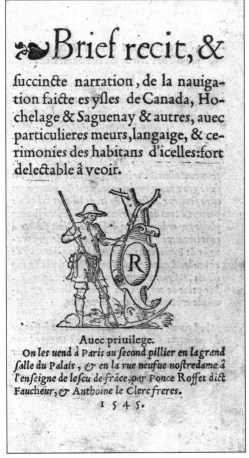

The 1545 title page of Jacques Cartier's Brief Recit, *an account of his travels in Canada with descriptions of the language and ceremonies of the inhabitants.*

An early historian of the American frontier once argued that "Spanish civilization crushed the Indian; English civilization scorned and neglected him; French civilization embraced and cherished him." He had a point. French settlers, eager to engage neighboring Indians in profitable trade and desperate for allies in wars with European rivals, developed much more harmonious relations with Indians than did either the Spanish or the English. It was the French settlers, more than any other Europeans, who were willing to learn the Native American languages, adopt Indian ways, and live with and marry into Indian families.

who had dealt with Champlain before met him again in 1608, they were eager to form an alliance. Champlain's account of the meeting offers a window into the rituals of negotiation preceding a formal alliance.

Pursuing our route, I met some two or three hundred savages, who were encamped in huts near a little island called St. Éloi, a league and a half distant from St. Mary. We made a reconnaissance, and found that they were tribes of savages, called Ochas teguins and Algonquins, on their way to Québec, to assist us in exploring the territory of the Iroquois, with whom they are in deadly hostility, sparing nothing belonging to their enemies.

After reconnoitering, I went on shore to see them, and inquired who their chief was. They told me there were two, one named Yroquet, and the other Ochas teguin, whom they pointed out to me. I went to their cabin, where they gave me a cordial reception, as is their custom.

I proceeded to inform them of the object of my voyage, with which they were greatly pleased. After some talk, I withdrew. Some time after, they came to my shallop [small boat], and presented me with some peltry, exhibiting many tokens of pleasure. Then they returned to the shore.

The next day, the two chiefs came to see me, when they remained some time without saying a word, meditating and smoking all the while. After due reflection, they began to harangue in a loud voice all their companions who were on the bank of the river, with their arms in their hands, and listening very attentively to what their chiefs said to them, which was as follows: that nearly ten moons ago, according to their mode of reckoning, the son of Yroquet had seen me, and that I had given him a good reception, and declared that . . . I desired to assist them against their enemies, with whom they had for a long time been at warfare, on account of many cruel acts committed by them against their tribe, under the color of friendship; that, having ever since longed for vengeance, they had solicited all the savages, whom I saw on the bank of the river, to come and make an alliance with us, and that their never having seen Christians also impelled them to come and visit us; that I should do with them and their companions as I wished; that they had no children with them, but men versed in war and full of courage, acquainted with the country and rivers in the land of the Iroquois; that now they entreated me to return to our settlement, that they might see our houses, and that, after three days, we should all together come back and engage in the war; that, as a token of firm friendship and joy, I should have muskets and arquebuses [harquebuses] fired, at which they would be greatly pleased. This I did, when they uttered great cries of astonishment, especially those who had never heard nor seen the like.

Over a century after Donnacona greeted Cartier, a very different scene took place on the Gaspé Peninsula. There a Micmac Indian elder, frustrated by French missionaries' efforts to convert his people to Christianity and by the French disdain for the Micmacs' home (which the French called "a little hell"), lectured a group of French settlers. Chrestien LeClerq, a missionary of the Recollect order, translated and recorded this speech around 1677.

I am greatly astonished that the French have so little cleverness. . . in the effort to persuade us to convert our poles, our barks, and our wigwams into those houses of stone and wood which are tall and lofty, according to their account as these trees. Very well! But why now, . . . do men of five to six feet in height need houses which are sixty to eighty? For, in fact, . . . do we not find in our own all the conveniences and the advantages that you have with yours, such as reposing, drinking, sleeping, eating, and amusing ourselves with our friends when we wish? This is not all, . . . my brother, hast thou as much ingenuity and cleverness as the Indians, who carry their houses and their wigwams with them so that they may lodge wheresoever they please, independently of any seignior whatsoever? Thou art not as bold nor as stout as we, because when thou goest on a voyage thou canst not carry upon thy shoulders thy buildings and they edifices. . . .

Thou reproachest us, very inappropriately, that our country is a little hell in contrast with France, which thou comparest to a terrestrial paradise, inasmuch as it yields thee, so thou sayest, every kind of provision in abundance. Thou sayest of us also that we are the most miserable and most unhappy of all men, living without religion, without manners, without honor, without social order, and, in a word, without any rules, like the beasts in our woods and our forests, lacking bread, wine, and a thousand other comforts which thou hast in superfluity in Europe. Well, my brother, if thou dost not yet know the real feelings which our Indians have toward thy country and toward all thy nation, it is proper that I inform thee at once. I beg thee now to believe that, all miserable as we seem in thine eyes, we consider ourselves nevertheless much hap-

Our young men will marry your daughters, and we shall be one people.
—Samuel de Champlain

The title page of Le Grand Voyage du Pays des Hurons *(The Great Voyage to the Country of the Hurons, 1632), an account by a French Catholic who lived at a mission in Canada. Images of the Huron Indians that appear at the top are possibly copied from descriptions provided by Samuel de Champlain.*

pier than thou in this, that we are very content with the little that we have; and believe also once for all, I pray, that thou deceivest thyself greatly if thou thinkest to persuade us that thy country is better than ours. For if France, as thou sayest, is a little terrestrial paradise, art thou sensible to leave it? And why abandon wives, children, relatives, and friends? Why risk thy life and thy property every year, and why venture thyself with such risk, in any season whatsoever, to the storms and tempests of the sea in order to come to a strange and barbarous country which thou considerest the poorest and least fortunate of the world? Besides, since we are wholly convinced of the contrary, we scarcely take the trouble to go to France, because we fear, with good reason, lest we find little satisfaction there, seeing, in our own experience, that those who are natives thereof leave it every year in order to enrich themselves on our shores.

The Society of Jesus

On one of Jacques Cartier's early voyages he wrote of the Indians, "We perceived that they are people who would be easy to convert." The charter for the Company of New France, written in 1602, was equally optimistic: "The Savages who will be led to the faith and to profess it will be considered natural Frenchmen, and like them, will be able to come and live in France when they wish to, and there acquire property, . . . just as if they had been born Frenchmen." But converting Native Americans to Christianity, and to French culture, was not so easy. Not only did the Indians cling to their own religious traditions, but the conditions under which Jesuit missionaries had to labor were less than ideal. (Jesuits are members of the religious order known as Society of Jesus; because of their characteristic clothing the Indians simply called them the Black Robes.) In 1697, the Jesuit missionary François de Crepieul, who had spent over a quarter century as a missionary in New France, left the following detailed note for his successors, "for their instruction and greater consolation," warning them of the sacrifices they would make while living and traveling with the Montagnais Indians and, less directly, expressing his scorn for Montagnais ways.

You tell us fine stories, and there is nothing in what you say that may not be true; but that is good for you who come across the seas. Do you not see that, as we inhabit a world so different from yours, there must be another heaven for us, and another road to reach it?

—A Huron Indian questioning Jean de Brébeuf, a Jesuit missionary (1635)

The Life of a Montagnaix Missionary is a Long and slow Martyrdom:

Is an almost continual practice of patience and of Mortification:

Is a truly penitential and Humiliating life, especially in the cabins, and on journeys with the Savages.

1. The cabin is made of poles and Birch-bark; and Fir-Branches are placed around it to cover the Snow and The frozen Ground.

2. During nearly all the day, The Missionary remains in a sitting or kneeling position, exposed to an almost continual smoke during The Winter.

3. Sometimes he perspires in the day-time and most frequently it is cold during The Night. He sleeps in his clothes upon The frozen Ground, and sometimes on the Snow covered with Fir-Branches, which are very hard.

4. He eats from an ourgan (dish) that is very seldom clean[ed] or washed, and in most cases is wiped with a greasy piece of skin, or is Licked by The dogs. He eats when there is anything to eat, and when some is offered to him. Sometimes The meat is only half-cooked; Sometimes it is very tough, especially when Smoked (dried in the smoke). . . .

5. The savage Shoes, or the dogs' hairy skins, serve him as napkins, as the hair of the Savage men and women serves them.

6. His usual Beverage is water from the Streams or from some pond—sometimes melted snow, in an ourgan that is usually quite greasy.

7. He often scorches his clothes, or his blanket, or his stockings during the Night. . . .

8. He always sleeps with his clothes on, and takes off his cassock and his Stockings only to protect himself against vermin, which always swarm on the Savages, especially the Children.

9. Usually when he wakes he finds himself surrounded by dogs. I have sometimes had 6, 8, or 10 around me.

10. The smoke is sometimes so strong that it makes his eyes weep; and when he sleeps he feels as if some one had thrown salt into his eyes. . . .

11. When the Snow Thaws, while he is walking upon Lakes or long Rivers, he is so dazzled for 4 or 5 days by the water that drops continually from his eyes that he cannot read his Breviary. Sometimes he has to be led by the hand. . . .

New World Jesuits

Jesuit priests learned native languages in order to better bring their religious message to the Iroquois and Algonquian peoples they sought to convert to Christianity. In an assembly on the shores of Lake Onondaga in 1656, Father Pierre Chaumonot gave the following speech in which he sought to explain the Jesuits' mission to a group of Iroquois, in their own language:

For the Faith, we have departed from our country; for the Faith, we have abandoned our relatives and our friends; for the Faith, we have crossed the Ocean; for the Faith, we have left behind the great ships of the French to set off on your small canoes; for the Faith, we have relinquished our fine houses to live in your bark cabins; for the Faith, we have deprived ourselves of our natural nourishment and the delicious foods that we could have enjoyed in France to eat your boiled meal and your other victuals, which the animals of our country would hardly touch.

Old World Germs

In 1640, a Huron woman, "one of the oldest and most notable of that nation," advised her village to reject the Jesuits' preaching, and suggested, even, that the Black Robes be put to death. She, like many native men and women, rightly suspected that the Jesuits had brought with them the terrible diseases that were taking the lives of her people. Although this speaker attributed the disease to spells cast by the Jesuits, the real source of contamination was Old World germs, inadvertently brought to the Indians by Jesuits.

It's the Black Robes who are making us die by their spells. Listen to me, I will prove it by reasons that you will recognize as true. They set themselves up in a village where everyone is feeling fine; no sooner are they there but everyone dies except for three or four people. They move to another place, and the same thing happens. They visit cabins in other villages, and only those where they have not entered are exempt from death and illness. Don't you see that when they move their lips in what they call prayer, spells are coming out of their mouths? It's the same when they read their books. They have big pieces of wood in their cabins [guns] by which they make noise and send their magic everywhere. If they are not promptly put to death, they will end up ruining the country, and no one will be left, young or old.

12. He is often annoyed by little Children, by their cries, their weeping, etc.; and sometimes he is made ill by the stench of those who have Scrofula, with whom he even Drinks out of the same kettle. . . .

13. He is sometimes reduced to drinking only water obtained from melted snow, which smells of smoke and is very dirty. . . .

14. In the summer-time, while Traveling, especially on The Saguenay and on the Great River, he often drinks the very dirty water obtained from Ponds. . . .

15. In most cases during the winter, while on long and difficult journeys, he does not find a drop of water wherewith to quench his thirst, although exhausted with toils and fatigues.

16. He suffers greatly from cold and from smoke, before the Cabin is finished, for 2 or 3 hours when the Weather is very severe in winter. His shirt, which is wet with perspiration, and his soaked stockings, render him Benumbed with cold; he suffers also from Hunger, because in most cases he has had nothing but a piece of dried meat, eaten before the camp was struck.

17. Suffering and hardship are the appanages [companions] of these holy but arduous Missions. *Faxit Deus ut iis diu immoretur et immoriatur Servus Inutilis Missionum Franciscus, S. J.* (God grant that in them may long remain and die the Useless Servant of the Missions, François, S. J.).

Among the greatest martyrdoms a Jesuit missionary might expect to endure was captivity by the Iroquois. Traditionally, the Iroquois practiced intermittent, brief "mourning wars," during which they compensated for deaths within their own community by taking captives and adopting them into the tribe. By the time Jesuits like François-Joseph Bressani arrived on the scene in 1642, however, so many Iroquois had died that the mourning wars had to be waged almost constantly in order to repopulate the League. By 1657, the same year Bressani made his map, the Jesuit missionary Paul le Jeune could claim that the Five Nations had absorbed so many captives that they were now made up of "more Foreigners than natives of the country."

When the Jesuit missionary Isaac Jogues was taken captive in 1643 by the Iroquois, he was subjected to a series of

brutal tortures, including the amputation of several fingers. In the following letter, written while he was still a captive, Jogues reflected on the military strength of the Iroquois and their potential for conversion to Christianity. He is especially sympathetic to some of his fellow captives, Huron (Algonquian speaking) Indians who had converted to Christianity.

Monsieur, here is the 4th [letter] that I have written since I am with the Iroquois. Time and paper fail me to repeat here what I have already conveyed to you at great length. [Guillaume] Couture and I are still living. Henry (one of those young men who were taken at Montreal) was brought here the eve of Saint John's day. He was not loaded with blows from clubs at the entrance to the village, like us, nor has he had his fingers cut, like us. He lives, and all the Hurons brought with him into the country. Be on your guard everywhere; new bands are always leaving, and we persuade ourselves that, until the Autumn, the river is not without enemies. There are here nearly three hundred arcquebuses [harquebuses], and seven hundred Iroquois; they are skilled in handling them. They can arrive at the three rivers by various streams; the Fort of Richelieu gives them a little more trouble, but does not hinder them altogether. . . . Quite recently there has departed a band, and the man of Mathurin (Father Brébeuf knows him well) is in it, and leads the band, as at our capture last year. This troop desires, and purposes to take some French, as well as Algonquins. Let not regard for us prevent [you] from doing that which is to the glory of God. The design of the Iroquois as far as I can see, is to take if they can, all the Hurons; and, having put to death the most considerable ones and a good part of the others, to make of them both but one people and only one land. I have a great compassion for these poor people, several of whom are Christians—the others Catecheumens (neophytes still receiving instruction), and ready for baptism; when shall a remedy be applied to these misfortunes? When they shall all be taken? I have received several letters from the Hurons, with the Relation taken near Montreal. The Dutch have tried to ransom us, but in vain; they are still endeavoring to do so at present, but it will again be,

White men show Native Americans an image of the Christian God in an attempt to convert them. The illustrator incorporates feather headdresses and trees that are not native to the region but does provide rough images of longhouses.

as I believe, with the same result. I become more and more resolved to dwell here as long as it shall lease Our Lord, and not to go away, even though an opportunity should present itself. My presence consoles the French, the Hurons, and the Algonquins. I have baptized more than sixty persons, several of whom have arrived in Heaven. That is my single consolation, and the will of God, to which very gladly I unite my own. I beg you to recommend that prayers be said, and that masses be offered for us, and above all for the one who desires to be forever,
MONSIEUR,

Your very humble servant, Isaac Jogues, of the Society of JESUS.

From the village of the Iroquois, the 30th of June, 1643.

New Worlds, New Women

LA MERE MARIE DE L'INCARNATION.
Premiere Superieure des Ursulines de la nouvelle france decedée a Quebec en odeur de Saintetè le dernier jour d'avril 1672. ageé de 72 ans 6 mois 13 i:

This portrait commemorates the death of Marie Guyart de l'Incarnation on the last day of April, 1672, aged 72 years, 6 months, and 13 days.

The changes in culture, social structure, and environment that were occasioned by encounters between Europeans and Native Americans had profound effects on the lives of women from both sides of the Atlantic. Often, women themselves determined and shaped those changes. Marie Guyart de l'Incarnation, a French nun of the Ursuline order, and Kateri Tekakwitha, an Algonquian convert to Christianity, lived within a few hundred miles of one another in 17th-century New France. Though the two women never met, their stories tell us a great deal about the choices women made in negotiating New World encounters.

Marie Guyart de l'Incarnation was born in Tours, France, in 1599. Her father was a baker. When Marie was 17, he arranged for her to marry a silkmaker named Claude Martin. By the age of 18, Marie had become a mother, by 19 a widow. After her husband's death, Guyart, who had always been a devout Catholic, became even more pious, dedicating her life to Jesus Christ and refusing to remarry. She began to read about the lives of saints and to imitate their devotions, which included many acts of "self-mortification." She attempted to "discipline her flesh" by beating herself with nettles and chains, wearing a hair shirt, and sleeping on a plain bed of boards, deprivations meant to bring her closer to Christ. As she put it, "I treated my body like a slave." Guyart took vows of chastity, obedience, and poverty and, when eventually ordained as an Ursuline nun,

took the name de l'Incarnation. She sought further trials of her devotion to Christ until, in 1639, she embarked on a voyage to Canada to establish a convent and school in Québec for Indian girls, whom she called *filles sauvages* (savage girls).

As Mother Superior of the Ursuline convent just outside the city of Québec, Marie de l'Incarnation's work included teaching young Iroquois and Algonquian girls the elements of the Catholic faith, with its catechism, prayers, and rituals. Yet she also learned from her students, studying Algonquian, Montagnais, and Huron to become fluent enough to write prayer books in those languages. Guyart enjoyed this work and became fascinated by what she saw as a fundamental similarity between the French and the Indians: their equal capacity to become Christians. As she wrote in 1640: "They are so attentive to what they are taught that . . . if I wanted to go over the catechism with them from morning till night, they would submit to it voluntarily. I am overcome with astonishment; I have never seen girls in France so ardent to be instructed and to pray God as they."

After founding the convent, Marie de l'Incarnation never left its confines again, except for a few weeks when it was being rebuilt after a fire in 1650 and for a few days once when there was danger of an Iroquois attack. She died at the convent in 1672. Her greatest regret was that she had failed recruit any of the *filles sauvages* to remain in the convent permanently, having convinced none to take the same vows that had shaped her own life.

If Marie de l'Incarnation had lived just a few years longer, she might well have met a young Algonquian woman who desired nothing more than to live the life of an Ursuline nun. Kateri Tekakwitha was born in the Mohawk village of Gandaouague, near present-day Québec, in 1656. Her mother was an Algonquian who had been converted by Jesuits at Three Rivers (perhaps Father Bressani himself baptized her), but her father, a Mohawk, was hostile to the new religion. When Kateri was four, a smallpox epidemic decimated her village, killing both her parents and leaving her with facial scars and weak vision. When Jesuits came to visit Gandaouague in her youth, Kateri listened to their preaching with rapture and, in 1676,

Everything concerning the study of the languages and the instruction of the Savages . . . has been so delectable to me that I have almost sinned in loving it too much.
—Marie de l'Incarnation

A 19th-century painter reconstructed this image of the appearance of the Ursuline convent in Quebec before it was destroyed by fire in 1650.

Kateri Tekakwitha was raised in a culture in which women wielded a great deal of political power. In the Mohawk village where Kateri grew up, as in all traditional Iroquois communities, women elected the tribal council and also spoke at village, tribal, and league meetings. As one French Jesuit observed, "the women name the counselors, and often chuse persons of their own sex." If Kateri Tekakwitha looked for symbols of women's power in the Black Robes' religion, it was probably because she cherished the authority women held in her native culture.

she was baptized. Like Marie de l'Incarnation, Kateri Tekakwitha heard about the lives of women saints. She was so impressed by Saint Catherine of Siena in particular that she took that name at her baptism.

Soon after becoming baptized, Catherine left Gandaouague, where her Mohawk friends and relatives had begun to ridicule her faith, and moved to a town populated by converted Catholics, many of whom had left their Iroquois villages for the same reason she had. In this town, Kahnawake, Catherine became an even more fervent Christian and, like Marie de l'Incarnation, began to emulate the lives of saints by practicing self-mortification. Also like de l'Incarnation, she refused to marry, claiming that she could "have no other spouse but Jesus Christ." And Catherine, too, sought further expressions of her faith: she and several other native women formed a group modeled after the Ursuline convent at Québec. In 1680, at the age of 24, weakened by her impassioned self-mortification (which included walking barefoot in ice and snow, burning her feet with a hot brand, and mixing ashes in her food), Kateri Tekakwitha died at Kahnawake. Soon after her death, two Jesuit priests wrote the story of her life to celebrate her martyrdom. Even today, Catholics make pilgrimages to Kahnawake to visit her relics. She may soon be canonized, officially decreed a saint, and thereby become the first Native American saint in the Catholic Church.

While Kateri Tekakwitha's early biographers celebrated her devout Christianity, she and other native converts may have seen their spirituality instead as a rich mixture of Christian and Iroquois beliefs. Many elements of Roman Catholicism were compatible with traditional Iroquois religion. For instance, the Holy Family—headed, in effect, by Mary and her mother, St. Anne, with Joseph only a distant figure—mirrored the Iroquois matrilineal [headed by women] society. The ancient Iroquois creation story cited in an earlier chapter about the Sky Woman who landed on Turtle's back and gave birth to all the descendants of the world, features an "Immaculate Conception" not unlike the story of the Virgin Mary. And the Catholic practice of fingering rosary beads has much in common with some Indian ritual uses of strings of wampum beads. Perhaps Tekakwitha herself saw Catholic rituals as a source of real or symbolic power, especially for women. She may even have experienced her own baptism as simultaneously a Catholic sacrament and a ritual "quicken-ing," an Iroquois practice in which water signals the symbolic rebirth of a deceased loved one. If so, by taking the name of St. Catherine of Siena, Kateri obliged herself to not only to imitate that medieval ascetic but to take on her identity and follow her model of physical deprivation. Or, like many Indi-ans whom the Jesuits believed had converted to Christianity, Tekakwitha may instead have been simply incorporating Catholic ideas and rituals into her own traditional beliefs, cre-ating a new hybrid blending New and Old World religions.

Covenants of War and Peace

France was not the only European country engaged in the northern fur trade. Beginning in 1621, the Dutch West India Company entered the fray. New Amsterdam and New Netherlands competed with New France for trading partner-ships. While the Dutch traded principally with the Mohawks and the French with the Hurons, both sought alliances with the powerful Iroquois. In 1634, Harmen Meyndertsz van den Bogaert and several of his Dutch countrymen traveled into Iroquois country to seek an alliance. Much to Bogaert's con-sternation, however, the Iroquois proved themselves to be sophisticated negotiators.

In the afternoon one of the [Iroquois] councillors came to ask me what we were doing in his country and what we brought him for gifts. I said that we brought him nothing, but that we just came for a visit. However, he said that we were worth nothing because we brought him no gifts. Then he told how the French had traded with them here with six men and had given them good gifts; for they had traded in the aforementioned river last August of this year with six men. We saw there were good timber axes, French shirts, coats, and razors. And this councillor derided us as scoundrels, and said that we were worthless because we gave them so little for their furs. They said that the French gave them six hands of sewant [loose beads; wampum] for one beaver and all sorts of other things in addition.

While the Jesuit missionary Isaac Jogues attempted to preach to the Iroquois during his captivity, he and his fellow captive, Guillaume Cousture, were, in a sense, merely pawns in a larger story of Iroquois diplomacy. For the better part of

the 17th and 18th centuries, the Peoples of the Longhouse successfully pitted the French, Dutch, and English colonial powers
against one another. As suggested by the strength of the united Five Nations, the Peoples of the Longhouse were consum-
mate diplomats. The following excerpt, from *The Treaty of
Peace Between the French, the Iroquois, and Other Nations*,
was recorded by the Jesuit Barthelemy Vimont. It illustrates
the power of symbol and ritual in Iroquois diplomacy.

On the fifth day of July, the Iroquois prisoner who had been set at
liberty and sent back to his own country . . . made his appearance at Three Rivers accompanied by two men of note among
those people, who had been delegated to negotiate peace with
Onontio [the governor of New France] . . . , and all the French,
and all the Savages who are our allies.

A young man named Guillaume Cousture who had been taken
prisoner with Father Isaac Jogues, and who had since then
remained in the Iroquois country, accompanied them. As soon as
he was recognized all threw their arms around his neck; he was
looked upon as a man risen from the dead, who brought joy to all
who thought him dead,—or, at least, that he was in danger of
passing the remainder of his days in most bitter and cruel captivity. As soon as he landed, he informed us of the design of the three
Savages with whom he had been sent back. When the most
important of the three, named Kiotsaeton, saw the French and the
Savages hastening to the bank of the river, he stood up in the bow
of the Shallop [open boat] that had brought him from Richelieu
to the Three Rivers. He was almost completely covered with
Porcelain beads. Motioning with his hand for silence, he called
out: "My Brothers, I have left my country to come and see you. At
last I have reached your land. I was told, on my departure, that I
was going to seek death, and that I would never again see my
country. But I have willingly exposed myself for the good of
peace. I come therefore to enter into the designs of the French, of
the Hurons, and of the Alguonquins. I come to make known to
you the thoughts of all my country." When he had said this, the
Shallop fired a shot from a swivel gun, and the Fort replied by a
discharge from the cannon, as a sign of rejoicing . . .

[Kiotsaeton and the French captives are welcomed and entertained while awaiting the arrival of Onontio, the governor.]

Finally, Monsieur the Governor came from Québec to three
Rivers, and . . . gave audience to [the Ambassadors] on the
twelfth of July. This took place in the courtyard of the Fort, over

which large sails had been spread to keep off the heat of the Sun. Their places were thus arranged: on one side was Monsieur the Governor, accompanied by his people and by Reverend Father Vimont, Superior of the Mission. The Iroquois sat at his feet, on a great piece of hemlock bark. They had stated before the assembly that they wished to be on his side, as a mark of the affection that they bore to the French.

Opposite them were the Algonquins, the Montagnais, and the Attikamegues; the two other sides were closed in by some French and some Hurons. In the center was a large space, somewhat longer than wide, in which the Iroquois caused two poles to be planted, and a cord to be stretched from one to the other on which to hang and tie the words that they were to bring us,—that is to say, the presents they wished to make us, which consisted of seventeen collars of porcelain beads, a portion of which were on their bodies. The remainder were enclosed in a small pouch placed quite near them. When all had assembled and had taken their places, Kiotsaeton who was high in stature, rose and looked at the Sun, then cast his eyes over the whole Company; he took a collar of porcelain beads in his hand and commenced to harangue in a loud voice. "Onontio, lend me ear. I am the mouth for the whole of my country; thou listenest to all the Iroquois, in hearing my words. There is no evil in my heart; I have only good songs in my mouth. We have a multitude of war songs in our country; we have cast them all on the ground; we have no longer anything but songs of rejoicing." Thereupon he began to sing; his countrymen responded; he walked about that great space as if on the stage of a theatre; he made a thousand gestures; he looked up to Heaven; he gazed at the Sun; he rubbed his arms as if he wished to draw from them the strength that moved them in war.

In an engraving from 1577, Queen Elizabeth steers the ship of Europe, a symbol of the growing superiority of British sea power. The British would soon fight the French and Spanish for control of the American continent. The Greek letters around the border (beginning at the upper left) spell out the words "HIEROGLYPHICON BRITANICON," indicating that the symbols in the picture represent England's power over the world and Elizabeth's role as champion of the Christian faith.

Chapter Five

The English Arrive

When Arthur Barlowe's ship reached shallow waters off the coast of the Carolinas in 1584, he believed he had found a perfect site for an English settlement. "The air smelt as sweet and strong as if we were in a fragrant flower garden," he wrote to Sir Walter Raleigh, who had financed the voyage and to whom Queen Elizabeth had deeded rights to any new-found land. After sighting land, Barlowe cast anchor and, as he later told Raleigh, "We manned the boats and rowed to land, taking possession of it in the name of the Queen's Most Excellent Majesty. We proclaimed her rightful queen and ruler and then delivered it to your use according to Her Majesty's grant and letters patent under Her Highness's great seal." So began English colonial ventures in North America with this brief ceremony.

Yet, even as Barlowe and his men were exploring Roanoke, the island on which they had landed, its native inhabitants were cautiously eyeing the newcomers. On the third day, three Algonquian Indians reversed Barlowe's journey: in a small boat they rowed from the island out to Barlowe's ship. Soon the two peoples were exchanging food and clothing, and the Algonquian leaders, Wingina and Granganimeo, had invited the English sailors to visit their homes. Barlowe told Raleigh that "we were entertained with kindness and friendship and were given everything they could provide. We found these people gentle, loving, and faithful, lacking all guile and trickery." When the English left to return to England, they took with them tales of a rich and splendid land, populated with a generous and welcoming people. They also probably carried with them samples of Roanoke's plenty, its plants and animals. Most tellingly, they took with them two Algonquian Indians, Manteo and Wanchese.

It is difficult to know now just what Roanoke's native inhabitants made of Barlowe and his companions. During this first encounter the English were never hostile, but neither were they trusting. When a

Military Men

Sir Walter Raleigh, a favorite of Queen Elizabeth in his youth, was the man behind the scheme to plant an English colony in the Chesapeake Bay. This portrait of Raleigh, in which he holds a compass in his left hand and stands before a globe, emphasizes his vision of himself as an explorer and conqueror. Following the advice of Richard Hakluyt, Raleigh hoped to establish a military outpost in the New World from which to attack Spanish treasure fleets. But Roanoke, the colony Raleigh sponsored in 1584, was a dismal failure. One reason the colony failed was that Raleigh and others in England considered Spain the colony's main enemy, and did little to negotiate good relations with the local Algonquian Indians (one of whom is shown here in a portrait by John White). When the Roanoke settlers mounted guns on their fort walls, they faced the guns east, over the ocean, where they expected danger from Spanish ships. But the disappearance of all members of the colony, by 1590, may have had more to do with the danger they did not anticipate: deteriorating relations with local Indians.

group of Englishmen once visited Granganimeo's house, his wife expected them to stay the night, since the return journey to the ship was long and the weather had turned bad, but Barlowe and his men insisted on sleeping out of doors, without shelter, even though they were nervous and uncomfortable. Clearly mystified at this strange behavior, Granganimeo's wife nonetheless indulged her guests by providing them with mats to protect themselves from the rain. But such affronts to native hospitality did little to build good relations.

Nowhere is the possibility for misunderstanding better illustrated than in Barlowe's misconception that the Algonquian name for the country was Wingandacoa. In fact, win-gan-da-coa simply means "you wear fine clothes." Such misunderstandings probably plagued many of the interactions between the Englishmen and the Indians. When the English returned in April 1585 to establish a settlement, they brought back the Algonquians Manteo and Wanchese, who had over the last year learned English, and an Englishman, Thomas Hariot, who had learned the Indians' language. Yet, despite the assistance of these interpreters, two separate attempts to found an English colony on Roanoke failed utterly. (Towns named Manteo and Wanchese still exist today, however.) After leaving an apparently thriving colony of several hundred men, women, and children in 1587, John White returned in 1590 to find that the colony had simply vanished. A more permanent English colony would not be established in Virginia until 1607.

In describing the local Indians to Raleigh, Barlowe remarked, "It was as if they lived in a golden age of their own." Barlowe, like so many Europeans, saw only what he wanted to see. Ironically, from the Indians' own perspective, looking back at the time preceding the English arrival in Virginia, before Old World diseases decimated their society and the English came to dominate the land, Barlowe may have had a point—it may well have been a golden age.

Go West

While Barlowe and his men were exploring Roanoke, Richard Hakluyt, an English scholar, geographer, and ambassador, was composing an argument in favor of establishing English colonies in North America. In October 1584, Hakluyt presented his "Discourse on the Western Planting" to Queen Elizabeth. Hakluyt had spent much of 1583 in France, which led him to be especially conscious of England's need to compete with the French and Spanish colo-

nial ventures. Here is his list of 23 reasons to found an English colony in the New World.

A brefe Collection of certaine reasons to induce her Majestie and the state to take in hande the westerne voyadge and the plantinge there.

1. The soyle yeldeth and may be made to yelde all the severall commodities of Europe. . . .

2. The passage thither and home is neither to longe nor to shorte, but easie and to be made twise in the yere.

3. The passage cutteth not nere the trade of any Prince, nor any of their contries or Territories and is a safe passage, and not easie to be annoyed by Prince or potentate whatsoever.

4. The passage is to be perfourmed at all times of the yere. . . .

5. And where England nowe for certen hundredth yeres last passed by the peculiar commoditie of wolles [wool], and of later yeres by clothinge of the same, hath raised it selfe from meaner state to greater wealthe and moche higher honour, might and power then before. . . . It commeth nowe so to passe that by the greate endeavor of the increase of the trade of wolles in Spaine and in the west Indies nowe daily more and more multiplienge, That the wholles of England and the clothe made of the same, will become base . . . it behoveth this Realme . . . to plant at Norumbega or some like place . . . the principall and in effecte the onely enrichinge contynueinge naturall commoditie of this Realme. . . .

6. This enterprise may staye the spanishe kinge from flowinge over all the face of that waste firme of America. . . .

7. This voyadge [will lead to the production of] meane shippes of greate burden and of greate strengthe for the defence of this Realme, and for the defence of that newe seate, as nede shall require, and withall greate increase of perfecte seamen . . . .

8. This newe navie of mightie newe stronge shippes so in trade to that Norumbega and to the coastes there, shall never be subjecte to arreste of any prince or potentate, as the navie of this Realme from time to time hath bene in the portes of the empire. . . .

9. The greate masse of wealthe of the realme imbarqued in the-marchantes shippes caried oute in this newe course, shall not lightly in so farr distant a course from the coaste of Europe be driven by windes and Tempestes into portes of any forren princes. . . .

10. No forren commoditie that commes into England commes withoute payment of custome once twise or thrice before it come into the Realme, and so all forren commodities become derer to the subjectes of this Realme, and by this course to Norumbega forren princes customes are avoided, and the forren commodities cheapely purchased, they become cheape to the subjectes of England. . . .

11. At the firste traficque with the people of those partes, the subjectes of this Realme for many yeres shall chaunge many cheape commodities of these partes, for thinges of highe valour there not estemed, and this to the great inrichinge of the Realme, if common use faile not.

12. By the greate plentie of those Regions the marchantes and their factors shall lye there cheape, buye and repaire their shippes cheape, and shall returne at pleasure withoute staye or restrainte of foreigne Prince. . . .

13. By makinge of Cables and Cordage, by plantinge of vines and olive trees, and by makinge of wyne and oyle, by husbandrie and by thousandes of thinges there to be don, infinite nombers of the english nation may be sett on worke to the unburdenynge of the Realme with many that nowe lyve chardgeable to the state at home.

14. If the sea coste serve for makinge of salte, and the Inland for wine, oiles, oranges, lymons, figges &Yc., and for makinge of iron, all which with moche more is hoped, withoute sworde drawen, wee shall cutt the combe of the frenche, of the spanishe, of the portingale, and of enemies, and of doubtfull frendes to the abatinge of their wealthe and force, and to the greater savinge of the wealthe of the Realme.

15. The substaunces servinge, wee may oute of those partes receave the masse of wrought wares that now wee receave out of Fraunce, Flaunders, Germanye &c. . . .

16. Wee shall by plantinge there inlarge the glory of the gospell and from England plante sincere relligion, and provide a safe and a sure place to receave people from all partes of the worlde that are forced to flee for the truthe of gods worde.

17. If frontier warres there chaunce to aryse, and if thereupon wee shall fortifie, that will occasion the trayninge upp of our youth in the discipline of warr, and make a nomber fitt for the service of the warres and for the defence of our people there and at home.

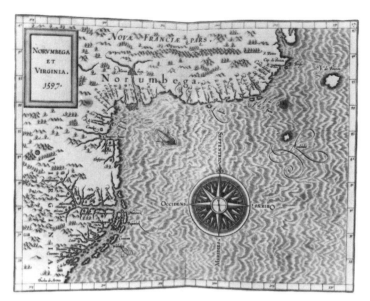

18. The Spaniards governe in the Indies with all pride and tyranie; and like as when people of contrarie nature at the sea enter into Gallies, where men are tied as slaves, all yell and crye with one voice *liberta, liberta*, as desirous of libertie or freedome, so no doubte whensoever the Queene of England . . . shall seate upon that firme of America, and shal be reported throughoute all that tracte to use the naturall people there with all human-itie, curtesie, and freedome, they will yelde themselves to her governement and revolte cleane from the Spaniarde. . . .

19. The present shorte trades causeth the maryner to be cast of, and ofte to be idle and so by povertie to fall to piracie: But this course to Norumbega . . . cutteth of the principall actions of piracie. . . .

20. Many men of excellent wittes and of divers singuler giftes overthrowen by suertishippe, by sea or by some folly of youthe, that are not able to live in England may there be raised againe, and doo their Contrie good service: and many nede-full uses there may (to great purpose) require the savinge of greate nombers that for trifles may otherwise be devoured by the gallowes.

21. Many souldiers and servitours in the ende of the warres that might be hurtfull to this Realme, may there be unladen, to the common profite and quiet of this Realme, and to our forreine benefite there as thye may be employed.

22. The frye of the wandringe beggars of England that growe upp idly and hurtefull and burdenous to this Realme, may

Whither Norumbega?

Richard Hakluyt urged the English settlers "to plant at Norumbega or some like place"—but where exactly was Norumbega? Was it really a place? Or was it yet another European myth, like the elusive Fountain of Youth? It was both. Beginning in the 1520s, Europeans used "Norumbega" to refer to a place where they expected to find a terrestrial paradise. The place was real, the paradise a wishful fantasy. Sixteenth-century maps of North America commonly used the designation Norumbega to label an area of the northeastern coast of North America stretching from New York to Newfoundland. Writings from the same period used Norumbega to name a wondrous king-dom full of untold riches to be found just a few miles inland from the Atlantic. In 1545, one French writer exulted that "the land over-flows with every kind of fruit; there grow the wholesome orange and the almond, and many sorts of sweet-smelling trees. The country is called by its people Norumbega." David Ingram, an Englishman who claimed to have walked all the way to Norumbega after being shipwrecked along the Gulf of Mexico in 1567, claimed that he found there "a towne half a myle long" with "many streets farr broader than any street in London" and people dressed in gold, silver, and jewels. Tales like Ingram's fired the imaginations of countless English and French explorers, who, as it hap-pened, found in Norumbega not gold but a wealth of fishes and furs.

there be unladen, better bredd upp, and may people waste Contries to the home and forreine benefite, and to their owne more happy state.

23. If England crie oute and affirme that there is so many in all trades that one cannot live for another as in all places they doe, This Norumbega (if it be thoughte so goodd) offreth the remedie.

Roanoke, the Lost Colony

A year after Arthur Barlowe returned from his reconnaissance of Roanoke Island, an expedition was sent to the island to found a colony. After establishing a fort on Roanoke, the colony's governor, Ralph Lane, wrote to Richard Hakluyt (the cousin of the man with the same name who wrote the "Discourse on the Western Planting") to inform him of the colony's progress. The letter emphasizes the land's tremendous promise, yet, like much of the correspondence from the early colonies, it also indulges in a good deal of hyperbole.

We have discovered the maine[-land] to bee the goodliest soile under the cope [vault] of heaven, so abounding with sweete trees, that bring such sundry rich and most pleasant gummes, grapes of such greatnes, yet wild, as France, Spaine nor Italy hath no greater, so many sortes of Apothecarie drugs, such severall kindes of flaxe, and one kind like silke, the same gathered of a grasse, as common as grasse is here. And now within these few dayes we have found here a Guinie wheate, whose eare yeeldeth corne for bread, 400.l upon one eare, and the Cane maketh very good and perfect suger. . . Besides that, it is the goodliest and most pleasing territorie of the world (for the soile is of an huge unknowen greatnesse, and very wel peopled and towned, though savagelie) and the climate so wholesome, that we have not had one sicke, since we touched land here. To conclude, if Virginia had but Horses and Kine [cattle] in some reasonable proportion, I dare assure my self being inhabited with English, no realme in Christendome were comparable to it. For alreadie we find, that what commodities soever Spaine, France, Italy, or the East parts do yeeld unto us in wines of all sortes, in oiles, in flaxe, in rosens, pitch, frankenscence, currans, sugers, & such like, these parts do abound with the growth of them all, but being Savages that possesse the land, they know no use of the same. And sundry other rich commodities, that no parts of the world, be they West or East Indies, have, here we finde great abundance of. The people naturally most curteous, & very desirous to have clothes, but especially of course cloth rather than silke, course canvas they also like wel of, but copper carieth the price of all, so it be made red. . . . From the new Fort in Virginia, this 2 September 1585. Your most assured friend, Rafe Lane.

To better document the riches of England's new territories, a painter, John White, and a scientist, Thomas Hariot, were sent on the early Roanoke voyages. White's watercolors and Hariot's detailed *Briefe and True Report of the New Found Land of Virginia* are some of the most valuable descriptions of Native American life.

John White returned to Roanoke in 1587, this time as governor of the colony. His journal from that expedition documents the increasing hostilities between the Algonquian Indians and the English settlers. In this excerpt, White relates one of the English colonists' more devastating mistakes: inadvertently attacking and killing some of their own Indian allies.

The next day, being the ninth of August, in the morning so earely, that it was yet darke, wee landed neere the dwelling place of our enemies, and very secretly conveyed our selves through the woods, to that side, where we had their houses betweene us and the water: and having espied their fire, and some sitting about it, we presently sette on them: the miserable soules herewith amassed, fledde into a place of thicke reedes, growing fast by, where our men perceaving them, shotte one of them through the bodie with a bullet, and therewith wee entered the reedes, among which wee hoped to acquite their evill doing towards us, but wee were deceaved, for those Savages were our friends, and were come from Croatan, to gather the corne, and fruite of that place, because they understoode our enemies were fledde immediately after they had slaine George Howe, and for haste had left all

&❧ A briefe and true re-
port of the new found land of Virginia: of
the commodities there found and to be raysed, as well mar-
chantable, as others for victuall, building and other necessa-
rie vses for those that are and shalbe the planters there; and of the nature and manners of the naturall inhabitants : Discouered by the
English Colony there seated by Sir Richard Greinuile *Knight in the*
yeere 1585. which remained vnder the gouernment of Rafe Lane Esqui-
er, one of her Maiesties Equieres, during the space of twelue monethes : at
the speciall charge and direction of the Honourable SIR
WALTER RALEIGH Knight, Lord Warden of
the stanneries ; who therein hath beene fauou-
red and authorised by her Maiestie and
her letters patents:

Directed to the Aduenturers, Fauourers,
*andWelwillers of the action, for the inhabi-
ting and planting there:*

By *Thomas Hariot*; seruant to the abouenamed
Sir Walter, *a member of the Colony, and
there imployed in discouering.*

Imprinted at London 1588.

The title page of A Briefe and True Report of the New Found Land of Virginia.

Thomas Hariot published his Briefe and True Report of the New Found Land of Virginia *in 1588, after spending almost a year there. He achieved international fame with its publication. In this portrait, his hand resting on the globe indicates his mastery over the New World.*

their corne, Tabacco, and Pompions [pumpkins] standing in such sorte, that all had beene devoured of the birdes, and Deere, if it had not beene gathered in time: but they had like to have paide deerely for it: for it was so darke, that they beeing naked, and their men and women apparelled all so like others, we knewe not but that they were all men: and if that one of them, which was a Weroans wife, had not had her childe at her backe, she had been slaine in steede of a man. . . . Finding our selves thus disappointed of our purpose, wee gathered all the corne, pease, Pumpions, and Tabacco, that we found ripe, leaving the rest unspoiled, and tooke Menatoan his wife, with the yong childe, and the other Savages with us over the water to Roanok. Although the mistaking of these Savages somewhat grieved Manteo, yet he imputed their harm to their owne follie.

While many reports from Roanoke, like Ralph Lane's, spoke of the colony in glowing terms, rumors of dissension and fractiousness among the colonists there soon made it back to England. More damaging still, some returning colonists disparaged the land itself. Thomas Hariot was recruited to write an account to dispel these rumors. In this excerpt, he attacks those who would speak ill of the English ventures.

Of our companie that returned some for their misdemeanour and ill dealing in the countrey, have bene there woorthily punished, who by reason of their bad natures, have maliciously not onely spoken ill of their Governours, but for their sakes slaundered the countrey it selfe. . . .

Some being ignorant of the state thereof, notwithstanding since their returne amongst their friends and acquaintaces, and also others, especially if they were in companie where they might not be gainsayd, would seeme to know so much as no men more, and make no men so great travellers as themselves. They stoode so much, as it may seeme, upon their credite and reputation, that having bene a twelve moneth in the countrey, it would have bene a great disgrace unto them as they thought, if they could not have sayd much whether it were true or false. Of which some have spoken of more than ever they sawe, or otherwise knew to be there. . . .

The cause of their ignorance was, in that they were of that many, that were never out of the Island where we were seated, or not farre, or at least wise in few places els, during the time of our abode in the countrey, or of that many, that after golde and silver was not so soone found, as it was by them looked for, had litle or no care of any other thing but to pamper their bellies, or of that many which had litle understanding, lesse discretion, and more tongue then was needfull or requisite.

Some also were of a nice bringing up, only in cities or townes, or such as never (as I may say) had seene the world before. Because there were not to be found any English cities, nor such faire houses, nor at their owne wish any of their old accustomed daintie food, nor any soft beds of downe or feathers, the countery was to them miserable, and their reports thereof according.

Powhatan and His People

After the English failure to establish a permanent settlement at Roanoke, lack of financial and political support delayed another attempt until 1607. In that year, English colonists settled at a site along the shores of Virginia that they named Jamestown after their king, James I. They had settled, however, at the heart of territory controlled by the Algonquian leader Powhatan, whose land included most of the Virginia coastal plain.

The deerskin cloak known as Powhatan's mantle (right), probably worn by Powhatan at ceremonial occasions, doubled as a map. A human figure at its center represents Powhatan himself, while the 34 circles around him correspond to the villages under his control. (In 1612 an English observer wrote that Powhatan's "petty Weroances [Indian chiefs] in all, may be in nomber, about three or fower and thirty.") The animals to the right and left of the human figure, a white-tailed deer and a wolf or mountain lion, may represent Powhatan's hunting prowess or a connection to animal spirits.

Although Powhatan had only recently consolidated his empire when the English settlers of 1607 arrived in Jamestown, he was nonetheless a leader to be reckoned with. John Smith, the leader of the Jamestown colony, sought alliances with Powhatan and his people—especially because the colony had to rely on the Indians' assistance for food—but relations often deteriorated into violence. Here, Powhatan explains the Indians' many frustrations with the English settlers.

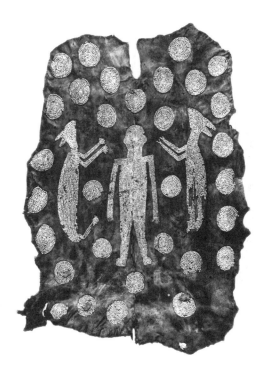

Powhatan's mantle, or cloak, was made of deer hide. A human figure with an animal on either side decorates the outside.

Marche du Calumet de Paix

The chief of the Natchez people leads a procession carrying a ceremonial peace pipe called a calumet to the Europeans waiting in the shelter. The Native American ceremony was a gesture of good will toward the Europeans.

Captain Smith you may understand, that I, having seene the death of all my people thrice, and not one living of those 3 generations, but my selfe, I knowe the difference of peace and warre, better then any in my Countrie. But now I am old, and ere long must die, my brethren, namely Opichapam, Opechankanough, and Kekataugh, my two sisters, and their two daughters, are distinctly each others successours, I wish their experiences no lesse then mine, and your love to them, no lesse then mine to you; but this brute [news] from Nansamund that you are come to destroy my Countrie, so much affrighteth all my people, as they dare not visit you; what will it availe you, to take that perforce, you may quietly have with love, or to destroy them that provide you food? what can you get by war, when we can hide our provision and flie to the woodes, whereby you must famish by wronging us your friends; and whie are you thus jealous of our loves, seeing us unarmed, and both doe, and are willing still to feed you with that you cannot get but by our labors? think you I am so simple not to knowe, it is better to eate good meate, lie well, and sleepe quietly with my women and children, laugh and be merrie with you, have copper, hatchets, or what I want, being your friend; then bee forced to flie from al, to lie cold in the woods, feed upon acorns, roots, and such trash, and be so hunted by you, that I can neither rest, eat, nor sleepe; but my tired men must watch, and if a twig but breake, everie one crie there comes Captaine Smith, then must I flie I knowe not whether, and thus with miserable feare end my miserable life; leaving my pleasures to such youths as you, which through your rash unadvisednesse, may quickly as miserably ende, for want of that you never knowe how to find? Let this therefore assure you of our loves and everie yeare our friendly trade shall furnish you with corne, and now also if you would come in friendly manner to see us, and not thus with your gunnes and swords, as to invade your foes.

Founding Jamestown

From the very start, Jamestown was a colony with problems. In 1607, 144 settlers set out on the voyage to Virginia, but 40 died of disease before ever reaching America. When they finally did arrive, in May, they chose an ill-suited site on a swampy peninsula. By January 1608, all but 38 colonists had died. There were many reasons for this dramatic attrition, among them the fact that many of the colonists were English

gentlemen unskilled at agricultural labor. In 1608, John Smith imposed stiff rules on the colony, but even these measures could not halt the deterioration of the venture. By 1624, although 8,000 English men, women, and children had migrated to Virginia, all but 1,300 had died there.

Even though Virginia's woods were filled with game and its rivers teemed with fish, many colonists simply starved to death. When the winter of 1609–10 began, there were 500 colonists in Jamestown; by spring, only 60 survived. The English even resorted to cannibalism: one man killed his wife, chopped her into pieces, and ate her, while other colonists dug up graves and fed on corpses. Most Europeans' stories about cannibalism among Native Americans were purely fictitious, but the early history of Jamestown provides a chilling example of the real thing—not by the Indians, but among the English.

The colonists couldn't feed themselves largely because they were unwilling to plant corn. If the English did any planting at all, they planted tobacco, which could turn a profit. Although tobacco planting in the early years of the colony was limited, it would soon become the linchpin of the colony's success. John Rolfe, a Jamestown colonist, planted the first English tobacco crop in 1612. Two years later, the colony shipped 170 pounds of cured tobacco leaves to England to sell. By 1620, 20,000 pounds were shipped annually, and by 1630, the amount rose to 1.5 million pounds.

In those first, fragile years, Jamestown colonists expected the Algonquians to supply them with food. Powhatan and his people thus had good reason to be frustrated with Captain Smith and the Jamestown colonists.

In a letter to the treasurer and council of Virginia, John Smith expressed his frustration with the fractiousness of the Jamestown settlers and reasserted his own commitment to fierce, even brutal, leadership.

Right Honorable, etc.

I Received your Letter, wherein you write, that our minds are so set upon faction, and idle conceits in dividing the Country without your consents, and that we feed You but with ifs and ands, hopes, and some few proofes; as if we would keepe the mystery of the businesse to our selves: and that we must expresly follow your instructions sent by Captain Newport: the charge of whose voyage amounts to neare two thousand pounds, the which if we can-

Nay, so great was our famine, that a Salvage [savage] we slew, and buried, the poorer sort tooke him up againe and eat him, and so did divers one another boyled and stewed with roots and herbs: And one amongst the rest did kill his wife, powdered her, and had eaten part of her before it was knowne, for which hee was executed, as hee well deserved; now whether shee was better roasted, boyled, or carbonado'd, I know not, but of such a dish as powdered wife I never heard of.

—John Smith, on cannibalism among the English colonists at Jamestown during the winter of 1609–10

Everie man and woman duly twice a day upon the first towling of the Bell shall upon the working daies repaire unto the Church, to hear divine Service upon pain of losing his or her dayes allowance for the first omission, for the second to be whipt, and for the third to be condemned to the Gallies for six Moneths. Likewise no man or woman shall dare to violate or breake the Sabboth by any gaming, publique, or private abroad, or at home, but duly sanctifie and observe the same, both himselfe and his familie, by preparing themselves at home . . . as also every man and woman shall repaire in the morning to the divine service, and Sermons preached upon the Saboth day, and in the afternoon to divine service, and Catechising, upon paine for the first fault to lose their provision, and allowance for the whole weeke following, for the second to lose the said allowance, and also to be whipt, and for the third to suffer death.

—from "Lawes divine, morall and martiall" (Jamestown, 1611)

not defray by the Ships returne, we are like to remain as banished men. To these particulars I humbly intreat your Pardons if I offend you with my rude Answer.

For our factions, unlesse you would have me run away and leave the Country, I cannot prevent them: because I do make many stay that would els fly any whether. For . . . dividing the Country etc. What it was I know not, for you saw no hand of mine to it; nor ever dream't I of any such matter. That we feed you with hopes, etc. Though I be no scholer [scholar], I am past a schoole-boy; and I desire but to know, what either you, and these here doe know, but that I have learned to tell you by the continuall hazard of my life. I have not concealed from you any thing I know; but I feare some cause you to beleeve much more then is true. . . .

For the charge of this Voyage of two or three thousand pounds, we have not received the value of an hundred pounds. And for the quartred Boat to be borne by the Souldiers over the Falles, Newport had 120 of the best men he could chuse. If he had burnt her to ashes, one might have carried her in a bag; but as she is, five hundred cannot, to a navigable place above the Falles. And for him at the time to find in the South Sea, a Mine of gold . . . I told them was as likely as the rest. But during this great discovery of thirtie myles, . . . they had the Pinnace and all the Boats with them, but one that remained with me to serve the Fort. In their absence I followed the new begun workes of Pitch and Tarre, Glasse, Sope-ashes, and Clapboord, whereof some small quantities we have sent you. But if you rightly consider, what an infinite toyle it is in Russia and Swethland [Sweden?], where the woods are proper for naught els, and though there be the helpe of both man and beast in those ancient Commonwealths, which many an hundred yeares have used it, yet thousands of those poore people can scarce get necessaries to live, but from hand to mouth. And thou your Factors there can buy as much in a week as will fraught you a ship, or as much as you please; you must not expect from us any such matter, which are but a many of ignorant miserable soules, that are scarce able to get wherewith to live, and defend our selves against the inconstant Salvages: finding but here and there a tree fit for the purpose, and want all things els the Russians have. . . . Though there be fish in the Sea, foules in the ayre, and Beasts in the woods, their bounds are so large, they so wilde, and we so weake and ignorant, we cannot much trouble them. . . . When you send againe I intreat you rather send but thirty Carpenters, husbandmen, gardiners, fisher men, blacksmiths, masons, and diggers up of trees, roots, well provided; then a thousand of such as we have: for except wee be able both to lodge them, and feed them, the most will consume with wantof ncessaries before they can be made good for any thing. . . . For in our over-toyling our weake and unskilfull bodies, to satisfie this desire of present profit, we can scarce ever recover our selves from one Supply to another. And I humbly intreat you hereafter, let us know what we should receive, and not stand to the Saylers courtesie to leave us what they please, els you may charge us with what you will, but we not you with any thing. These are the causes that have kept us in Virginia, from laying such a foundation, that ere this might have given much better content and satisfaction; but as yet you must not looke for any profitable returnes: so I humbly rest.

To replenish the supply of laborers in Jamestown, the Virginia Company, which financed the expedition, recruited emigrants by posting broadsides in English towns and placing advertisements in that country's newspapers. Since the situation in Jamestown was so dire, promoters of the venture painted a picture of the colony that had little to do with reality. The advertisement on this page, created in 1991, parodies the original Virginia Company brochures.

While Richard Hakluyt's "Discourse on the Western Planting" provided the justification for the early English colonial ventures in Roanoke and Jamestown, the failure of those colonies inspired later writers to revise Hakluyt's arguments. In 1625, Francis Bacon, arguably the most important English philosopher of his day, composed an essay titled "Of Plantations." Here, Bacon is particularly critical of some of the mistakes made in the settlement of Jamestown, where many colonists starved to death because they were unable or

This parody of the original Virginia Company brochures was published by two modern scholars in the William and Mary Quarterly.

From the moment the gentle, southern breezes waft your pinnace to the verdant, gardenlike shore, you'll know this is where you belong. Jamestown Estates, where only a few are living a life those in England can hardly imagine.

Jamestown Estates—another proud project of the Virginia Company—combines the best in colonial living with the excitement, adventure, and opportunity for which the Virginia Company is famous.

At Jamestown Estates, your every need is provided for in an environment that shows how caring people can live in symbiotic dominance of nature. And only Jamestown Estates offers an exclusive low cholesterol meal plan, the Sure-Fit™ exercise program, and a unique "Friends Together" living arrangement. In all details, Jamestown Estates is designed with your peace and well-being in mind. Each of our charming, thatch-roofed cottages—which you will share with congenial, adventuresome people just like yourself (specially designed to maximize both privacy and interpersonal contact)—has a spectacular river view. At Jamestown Estates, nature itself invites you to relax, reflect, converse with new-found friends, and share stories of your New World experiences, while becoming the sort of person you've always wanted to be. But it's not all play at Jamestown Estates—not by a long shot. For Jamestown Estates offers one of the most active labor

Headright™ and Headright System™ are registered trademarks of the Virginia Company. Offer void where prohibited.

markets in the New World. Whatever you do, you can do it better here.

Our employment office has many people anxious to welcome you to our growing work force.

No single ad can tell you all the remarkable things you'll want to know about Jamestown Estates. Consider, however, some of these exceptionally valuable Jamestown Pluses:
• 24-hour security, palisaded grounds.
• Hunting, fishing right on premises. Native guides teach you to hunt like a lord.
• The Sotweed Garden Center—learn how to plant like a pro. No experience necessary.
• Regularly scheduled "Trash For Treasure" excursions to the nearby Pamunkey Flea Market. Come & "Meet the Chief."
• And, as a special bonus to those who visit Jamestown Estates soon, we are introducing a new program called the Headright System*—your chance to receive 50 acres of land just for bringing yourself (or someone you know) to experience this new world of opportunity.
• Coming with a group? Ask about our Particular Plantations™ Program. Build your private world right here in our new one.

Finally, for those who appreciate the phenomenal profit potential of New World investment, there is the chance to secure shares in the Virginia Company itself—a once in a lifetime opportunity—starting at just £10 12s. 6d. To find out more, contact your nearest friendly, knowledgeable Virginia Company Representative.

WALT WOODWARD
KAREN KUPPERMAN

A WHOLE NEW WORLD

unwilling to do the labor required to feed themselves. The differences between Hakluyt's treatise and Bacon's essay suggest how greatly England's vision of colonization had changed from 1584 to 1625.

Planting of countries is like planting of woods; for you must make account to lose almost twenty years' profit, and expect your recompense in the end: for the principal thing that hath been the destruction of most plantations hath been the base and hasty drawing of profit in the first years. . . . It is a shameful and unblessed thing to take the scum of people and wicked condemned men to be the people with whom you plant; and not only so, but it spoileth the plantation; for they will ever live like rogues, and not fall to work, but be lazy, and do mischief, and spend victuals, and be quickly weary, and then certify over to their country to the discredit of the plantation. The people wherewith you plant ought to be gardeners, ploughmen, labourers, smiths, carpenters, joiners, fishermen, fowlers, with some few apothecaries, surgeons, cooks, and bakers. In a country of plantation, first look about what kind of victual the country yields of itself to hand: as chestnuts, walnuts, pine-apples, olives, dates, plums, cherries, wild honey, and the like; and make use of them. Then consider what victual or esculent [edible] things there are which grow speedily and within the year; as parsnips, carrots, turnips, onions, radish, artichokes of Hierusalem, maize, and the like: for wheat, barley, and oats, they ask too much labour; but with pease and beans you may begin, both because they ask less labour, and because they serve for meat as well as for bread; and of rice likewise cometh a great increase, and it is a kind of meat. Above all, there ought to be brought store of biscuit, oatmeal, flour, meal, and the like in the beginning till bread may be had. For beasts or birds take chiefly such as are least subject to diseases and multiply fastest; as swine, goats, cocks, hens, turkeys, geese, house-doves, and the like. . . . For government, let it be in the hands of one, assisted with some council; and let them have commission to exercise martial laws, with some limitation; and above all, let men make that profit of being in the wilderness, as they have God always and his service before their eyes. . . . If you plant where savages are do not entertain them with trifles and gingles, but use them justly and graciously, with sufficient guard nevertheless; and do not win their favour by helping them to invade their enemies, but for their defence it is not amiss. . . . When the plantation grows to strength, then it is time to plant with women as well as with men; that the plantation may spread into generations, and not be pieced from without. It is the sinfullest thing in the world to forsake or destitute a plantation once in forwardness; for, besides the dishonour, it is the guiltiness of blood of many commiserable persons.

Pocahontas and Her Legacy

Chief Powhatan's favorite daughter, Matoaka, was born about 1595 and, as she grew, was nicknamed Pocahontas, "playful one." In 1612, when Pocahontas was about 17, she was kidnapped by English soldiers who took her to Jamestown, hoping to exchange her for English colonists being held by Powhatan's people. While a captive in Jamestown, Pocahontas was persuaded to convert to Christianity and marry an Englishman, John Rolfe, which she did in 1614. At this point, Matoaka took yet another name: Rebecca Rolfe. Soon afterward, Pocahontas, her husband, and their infant son traveled to England, where they were received at the court of King James I. Pocahontas became fatally ill, however, and died in England in 1617, the day before she planned to return to Virginia.

The marriage of Rolfe and Pocahontas was intended in part to improve relations between the English colonists at Jamestown and their Powhatan Indian neighbors. In the years since the founding of Jamestown, the colonists had become even more dependent on the Indians for food, with the Algonquians understandably less and less willing to provide it. Feeding all of Jamestown proved an extraordinary strain on native resources. More importantly, instead of cultivating friendly trading relations with the Algonquians, the colonists were intent on inspiring fear among them, and were prone to attack them at the least provocation. The marriage between Rolfe and Pocahontas did usher in a brief period of relatively peaceful relations, but finally, in 1622, a confederation of Algonquians revolted against the English, attacking several colonial settlements and killing 347 colonists.

In the following letter, written just before John Rolfe's marriage to Pocahontas in 1614, he asks for the blessing of Sir Thomas Dale, the governor of Virginia, on his intentions to wed her. Rolfe argues that he wishes to marry Pocahontas for the sake of her salvation—marrying a Christian will bring

A portrait of Pocahontas at age 20, while she was in London with her husband and son. She died at age 22 and was buried in England.

Pocahontas (right, standing) pleads with her father, Powhatan (seated, with crown), to spare Captain John Smith's life. This ceremony may have been a mock execution designed to allow Smith to become a surrogate father to Pocahontas and a legitimate member of the Algonquian community.

You did promise *Powhatan* what was yours should bee his, and he the like to you; you called him father being in his land a stranger, and by the same reason so must I doe you . . . Were you not afraid to come into my father Countrie, and caused feare in him and all his people (but mee) and feare you here I should call you father; I tell you then I will, and you shall call mee childe, and so I will bee fore ever and ever your Countrieman.

—Pocahontas's speech to John Smith when they met in England, imploring him to remember that, because of the adoption ceremony he underwent, he is still kin to her.

her closer to God—but also "for the good of this plantation."

Honorable Sir, and most worthy Governor:

When your leisure shall best serve you to peruse these lines, I trust in God the beginning will not strike you into a greater admiration than the end will give you good content. It is a matter of no small moment, concerning my own particular, which here I impart unto you, and which toucheth me so nearly as the tenderness of my salvation. . . .

Let therefore this, my well-advised protestation, which here I make between God and my own conscience, be a sufficient witness at the dreadful Day of Judgement (when the secret of all men's hearts shall be opened) to condemn me herein, if my chiefest intent and purpose be not to strive with all my power of body and mind in the undertaking of so mighty a matter—[in] no way led . . . with the unbridled desire of carnal affection, but [striving] for the good of this plantation, for the honor of our country, for the glory of God, for my own salvation, and for the converting to the true knowledge of God and Jesus Christ [of] an unbelieving creature, namely Pocahontas, to whom my hearty and best thoughts are, and have [for] a long time been, so entangled, and enthralled in so intricate a labyrinth, that I was even wearied to unwind myself thereout. . . .

For besides the many passions and sufferings which I have daily, hourly, yea, and in my sleep endured, even awaking me to astonishment, taxing me with remissness and carelessness, [with] refusing and neglecting to perform the duty of a good Christian, pulling me by the ear and crying, "why dost not thou endeavor to make her a Christian?" (and these have happened, to my greater wonder, even when she hath been furthest separated from me, which in common reason, were it not an undoubted work of God, might breed forgetfulness of a far more worthy creature)— besides, I say, the holy spirit of God hath often demanded of me, why I was created, if not for transitory pleasures and worldly vanities, but to labor in the Lord's vineyard . . . ? And if this be, as undoubtedly this is, the service Jesus Christ requireth of His best servant: woe unto him that hath these instruments of piety put into his hands and willfully despiseth to work with them. Likewise, adding hereunto her great appearance of love to me, her desire to be taught and instructed in the knowledge of God, her capableness of understanding, her aptness and willingness to receive any good impression, and also the spiritual, besides her own, incitements stirring me up hereunto.

What should I do? Shall I be of so untoward a disposition as to refuse to lead the blind into the right way? Shall I be so unnatural as not to give bread to the hungry? . . . Shall the base fear of displeasing the world overpower and withhold me from revealing unto man these spiritual works of the Lord, which in my meditations and prayers I have daily made known to Him? God forbid. . . .

And so I rest,
at your command, most willing
to be disposed of,
John Rolfe

At [John Smith's] entrance before [Powhatan], all the people gave a great shout. The Queene of Appamatuck was appointed to bring him water to wash his hands, and another brought him a bunch of feathers, instead of a Towell to dry them: having feasted him after their best barbarous manner they could, a long consultation was held, but the conclusion was, two great stones were brought before *Powhatan*: then as many as could layd hands on him, dragged him to them, and thereon laid his head, and being ready with their clubs to beate out his brains, *Pocahontas* the Kings dearest daughter, when no entreaty could prevaile, got his head in her arms, and laid her owne upon his to save him from death.

—John Smith's account of how, as he perceived it, Pocahontas saved his life when he thought Powhatan was about to execute him

The story of Pocahontas has been told many times over, in poems, plays, novels, and, most recently, in a Walt Disney animated film. In the contemporary painting made while she was in England, Pocahontas (alias Rebecca) wears the elegant, refined costume of an English gentlewoman. [See page 121] In the Disney version (right), Pocahontas has been remade into a beautiful, sensual child of nature. Disney's *Pocahontas*, like most 19th- and 20th-century retellings of Pocahontas's story, focuses not on her marriage to John Rolfe but on her relationship with another Englishman, Captain John Smith. Smith claimed that while he was held captive among the Virginian Algonquians in 1607, Powhatan was about to execute him when Pocahontas intervened and saved his life. But Pocahontas's supposed rescue of Smith was probably instead part of an elaborate Algonquian ritual, a mock execution in which Smith was being symbolically adopted into the Powhatan community. Pocahontas sponsored his incorporation into the kinship-based community as a sort of surrogate father or godfather. Re-creations of the story, like the Disney film, claim that Pocahontas "rescued" Smith because she was in love with him (even though she was only 11 or 12 at the time), an explanation that hides two truths: first, that Smith's life was never actually in danger, and second, that, even though Smith didn't know what they were, Pocahontas undoubtedly had reasons of her own for doing what she did.

Chapter Six

Africans in America

While many Europeans eagerly emigrated to the Americas in search of riches and new trade routes, Africans traveled across the Atlantic most often against their will. European colonial ventures—especially those involving large-scale crops like sugar, rice, indigo, tobacco, and cotton—required enormous amounts of labor, which was largely supplied by African slaves. From 1450 to 1900, between 12 and 20 million Africans were taken from their homes and sold into slavery in the New World. Ninety-five percent of those who survived the voyage arrived in Latin America, including the Caribbean; only 5 percent were destined for what is now the United States. In the New World, despite being subjected to innumerable hardships, Africans, whether slave or free, nonetheless forged strong communities of their own and created distinctive cultures as a result of encounters with new environments and peoples.

From the very beginning, Africans participated in European ventures in the Americas. Enslaved Africans accompanied early Spanish expeditions, helped build early French settlements, and, by 1619, were supplying labor to English colonies in Virginia. By 1650, Africans actually constituted the majority of new arrivals to the Americas, though African slave labor did not become widespread in British mainland colonies until after 1680. At the peak of the slave trade, in 1780, eighty thousand Africans per year crossed the Atlantic. (Until 1820, when European immigration expanded, five Africans were forcibly brought to the Americas for every European who migrated voluntarily.)

The story of the African slave trade and African slavery in the early Americas is one of gripping horrors, astonishing courage, and enduring legacies. At its heart is an Atlantic trade network whose origins can be traced to the Portuguese exploration of Africa in the 15th century. Northern African societies had long been in contact with both Europe

In this 1730 etching of the New York slave market a large crowd has gathered under the gazebo to bid on newly imported African slaves. Although colonial laws called "black codes" regulated the buying, selling, and marrying of slaves, slaveowners had unquestioned authority over their lives.

Most Africans brought to the New World came from West Africa, where Portuguese, and later English, French, and Dutch, traders tapped into the local trade routes. Many Africans were captured by other Africans in the interior of the continent and marched to the coast for sale to Europeans.

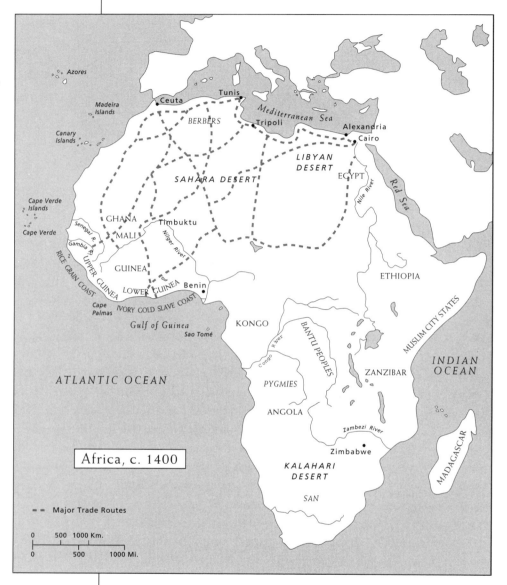

Africa, c. 1400

- - Major Trade Routes

and Asia, exchanging goods, languages, and religious and cultural practices. For example, many northern Africans were Muslims, having adopted the Arab religion of Islam. Contact with western Europe grew dramatically in the 1400s, however, when Portuguese traders developed new overland routes to northern Africa and new sea passages to that continent's western coast, an area Europeans called Guinea. Soon, Portuguese ships and caravans began exporting large numbers of Africans to western Europe as slaves.

Slavery had long been practiced in Europe, and the Africans brought by the Portuguese at first served alongside—but later gradually replaced—other enslaved peoples: Jews, Moors (the Arab conquerors of Spain), other Arabs, and eastern Europeans.

Slavery had also long been carried out in parts of Africa, where the local rulers of African city-states commonly enslaved their war captives. Portuguese merchants tapped the existing African trade networks and made use of their political ties to acquire slaves for Europe, but they soon found that the need for slave labor there was on the decline. More efficient agriculture contributed to an exploding population in 15th-century Europe, and that continent was beginning to be able to supply its own labor needs. At the same time, however, the need for workers in Europe's newfound colonies in the Americas was growing, so the Portuguese traders began taking their cargo across the Atlantic instead.

As the Atlantic slave trade grew, the forced transportation of Africans aboard westward-bound European ships (known as the middle passage) came to form just one strand of a complex web of trading routes connecting western Africa, western Europe, the Caribbean, and the Atlantic coast of North and South America. On southerly routes, ships from Europe brought manufactured goods from there—iron bars, textiles, firearms, and liquor—to the west coast of Africa. There, local merchants traded with the ships' captains, proffering slaves in exchange for goods. In Brazil, North America, and the Caribbean enslaved people were traded for plantation products like cotton, tobacco, indigo, and sugar, which were shipped back to Europe or other parts of the Atlantic world. Over time, European colonies, including British North America, increasingly sought the labor of enslaved Africans to produce large crops that brought enormous profits to an elite group of European and African merchants and helped to feed an expanding population in Europe. In 1663 one English trading corporation, the Company of Royal Adventurers, insisted to their king that "the trade of Africa is so necessary to England that the very being of the Plantations depends upon the supply of negro servants for their works."

Historians have long debated why it was that African slaves, rather than Native American or European servants, became the chief source of New World labor. There are several likely explanations, perhaps the most important being that slavery itself is dependent on preserving "we-they" distinctions. Whenever and wherever slavery has existed throughout history, the people who owned slaves have seen them as somehow different from themselves. Sometimes these differences have been about religion: Christians enslaved the Jews, Muslims enslaved the Christians. And often these differences have been about ethnicity, such as the Portuguese enslaving the Arabs. Where obvious differences did

In Benin, a 16th-century artisan cast this bronze relief of a West African warrior. Portuguese soldiers, with their superior weapons and armor, were able to defeat and enslave the Africans, and then used their long-established trade routes with Africa to round up slaves for the Americas.

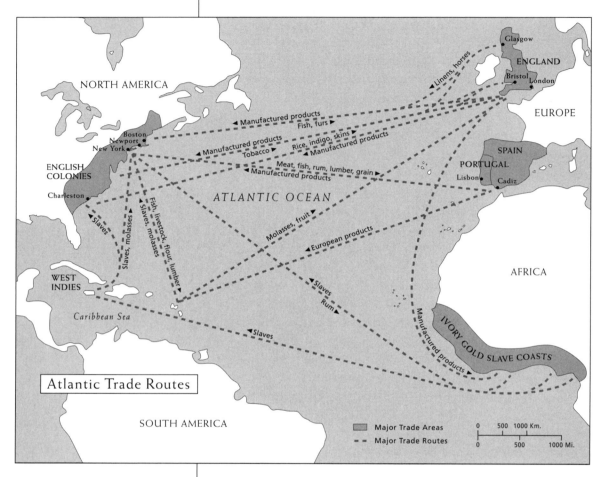

Atlantic Trade Routes

As the Atlantic slave trade expanded, it fueled a broad trade network involving raw materials (such as sugar and cotton) and manufactured goods (such as rum and linens).

not exist, they could be invented. Europeans had long perceived Africans as different from themselves, but in the 15th and 16th centuries Europeans increasingly came to define themselves as "white" and Africans as "black." Then, to this division they attached other meanings: white is good, black, bad; white is pure, black, impure. For example, in 1578 the Englishman George Best proposed this explanation for Africans' skin color: "The most probable cause . . . is, that this blacknesse proceedeth of some naturall infection of the first inhabitants of that Countrey [Africa], and so all the whole progenie of them descended, are still poluted with the same blot of infection." (Best believed that the indigenous inhabitants of the Americas were "not blacke, but white"—ideas about "redness" of Indians came later.)

The Europeans' ideas about differences between "whites" and "blacks," account at least in part for how they justified enslaving millions of African men, women, and children. Their thinking also explains why they rarely consigned Native Americans to that status and never forced other Europeans to come to the New World as slaves. But other factors may also have played a role. Native

Americans proved a poor source of labor, both because so many died of disease after exposure to European microbes and because, since they were natives, they could simply run away. European workers, meanwhile, often fell prey to tropical diseases, especially in the Caribbean and Latin America, and could easily run away and resettle elsewhere. Africans, however, had already been exposed both to Old World microbes like smallpox and tropical diseases like malaria and yellow fever. Unlike the Native Americans, Africans had few places to run to and, unlike the white Europeans, they could not simply blend in with European colonial society. Despite these obstacles, some runaway slaves did manage to found their own New World societies, like the black communities in Boston and Philadelphia in the 18th and 19th centuries, and the nation of Haiti, a country of former slaves who liberated themselves in a revolution in 1804.

However much more disease-resistant Africans were than their Native American and European counterparts, they still died in great numbers during the middle passage and during their first few months in the New World. About one in seven Africans died while on board ship, largely from dehydration, malnutrition, and abuse. Many more, weakened by the voyage, died within a few months of their arrival. Since more men than women were enslaved, Africans in the Americas were slow to reproduce. And, since slaves were taken from different parts of Africa and spoke various languages, many suffered severe isolation even within the slave communities. In many parts of the Americas, African-descended communities today speak hybrid languages, a sign of their innovative adaptation to New World conditions. Meanwhile, these same communities often effectively resisted the incursions of European cultures and maintained their characteristic African-derived arts and crafts traditions and religious practices. In 18th- and 19th-century British North America, free black communities would grow and thrive in northern towns like

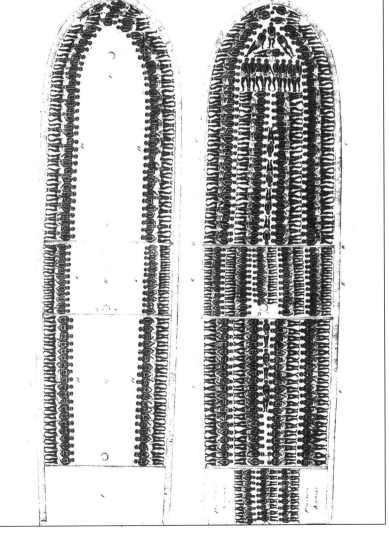

A diagram of a slave ship from a 1789 broadside reveals the cramped quarters that slaves endured during their passage across the Atlantic. Partly because of such crowded, unsanitary conditions, many Africans died on board.

Philadelphia and Boston. A handful of African Americans from that era have left us some of the richest stories imaginable—the stories of their own lives.

Kidnapped

Olaudah Equiano published his autobiography in 1789.

Olaudah Equiano was born in eastern Nigeria in 1745. When he was just 10 years old he was captured by African traders and taken far from home down the Niger River, toward the western coast of Africa. He lived and worked briefly as a slave to an African family but was eventually sold to European traders and carried across the Atlantic aboard a slave ship. Later in life, Equiano gained his freedom, learned to read and write, and traveled widely in Europe, the Americas, and even the Arctic. Equiano led an exceptional life. His freedom and his subsequent adventures were made possible through the intervention of several masters, through his own acquisition of literacy, and through his training as a sailor, an occupation with more liberties than most for Africans. This passage is from his autobiography, first published in 1789.

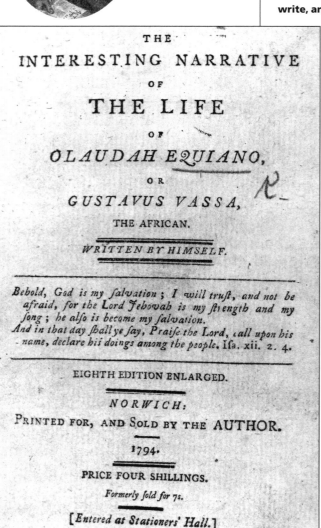

THE
INTERESTING NARRATIVE
OF
THE LIFE
OF
OLAUDAH EQUIANO,
OR
GUSTAVUS VASSA,
THE AFRICAN.

WRITTEN BY HIMSELF.

Behold, God is my salvation; I will trust, and not be afraid, for the Lord Jehovah is my strength and my song; he also is become my salvation. And in that day shall ye say, Praise the Lord, call upon his name, declare his doings among the people. Isa. xii. 2. 4.

EIGHTH EDITION ENLARGED.

NORWICH:
PRINTED FOR, AND SOLD BY THE AUTHOR.

1794.

PRICE FOUR SHILLINGS.

Formerly sold for 7s.

[*Entered at Stationers' Hall.*]

Generally when the grown people in the neighborhood were gone far in the fields to labor, the children assembled together to play, and commonly some of us used to get up a tree to look out for any assailant or kidnapper that might come upon us, for they sometimes took those opportunities of our parents' absence to attack and carry off as many as they could seize. One day, as I was watching at the top of the tree in our yard, I saw one of those people come into the yard of our next neighbor but one to kidnap, there being many stout young people in it. Immediately on this I gave the alarm of the rogue and he was surrounded by the stoutest of them, who entangled him with cords so that he could not escape till some of the grown people came in and secured him. But alas! ere long it was my fate to be thus attacked and carried off when none of the grown people were nigh. One day, when all our people were gone out to their works as usual and only I and my dear sister were left to mind the house, two men and a woman got over our walls, and in a moment seized us both, and without giving us time to cry out or make resistance they stopped our mouths and ran off with us into the nearest wood. Here they tied our hands and continued to carry us as far as they could till night came on, when we reached a small house where the robbers halted for refreshment and spent the night. We were then unbound but were unable to take any food, and being quite overpowered by fatigue and grief, our only relief was some sleep, which allayed our misfortune for a short time. . . . At length, after many days' traveling, during which I had often changed masters, I got into the hands of a chieftain in a very pleasant country. This man had two wives and some children, and they all used me extremely well and did all they could to comfort me, particularly the first wife, who was something like my mother. . . .

Equiano lived with this family for a brief time but was soon sold again. After a lengthy voyage he arrived at the coast, where he was taken to a slave ship.

I was soon put down under the decks, and there I received such a salutation in my nostrils as I had never experienced in my life: so that with the loathsomeness of the stench and crying together, I became so sick and low that I was not able to eat, nor had I the least desire to taste anything. I now wished for the last friend, death, to relieve me; but soon, to my grief, two of the white men offered me eatables, and on my refusing to eat, one of them held me fast by the hands and laid me across I think the windlass, and tied my feet while the other flogged me severely. I had never experienced anything of this kind before, and although, not being used to the water, I naturally feared that element the first time I saw it, yet nevertheless could I have got over the nettings I would have jumped over the side, but I could not; and besides, the crew used to watch us very closely who were not chained down to the decks, lest we should leap into the water. . . .

In a little time after, amongst the poor chained men I found some of my own nation, which in a small degree gave ease to my mind. I inquired to these what was to be done with us; they gave me to understand we were to be carried to these white people's country to work for them. I then was a little revived, and thought if it were no worse than working, my situation was not so desperate: but still I feared I should be put to death, the white people looked and acted, as I thought, in so savage a manner. . . . I could not help expressing my fears and apprehensions to some of my countrymen: I asked them if these people had no country but lived

I must own, to the shame of my own countrymen, that I was first kidnapped and betrayed by some of my own complexion, who were the first cause of my exile and slavery; but if there were no buyers there would be no sellers. So far as I can remember, some of the Africans in my country keep slaves, which they take in war, or for debt; but those which they keep are well fed, and good care taken of them, and treated well.

—Ottobah Cugoano, writing in 1787, recalling his capture near present-day Ghana

in this hollow place [the ship]: they told me they did not, but came from a distant one. "Then," said I, "how comes it in all our country we never heard of them?" They told me because they lived so very far off.

Tips for Slave Traders

The European merchants who funded Atlantic slave-trade ventures watched over their investments carefully, especially since the possibility for great losses—or huge profits—was considerable. Any delay in crossing the Atlantic only heightened the risk that the enslaved people carried as cargo would die of disease or dehydration, and the longer the trip, the more numerous the deaths. Isaac Hobhouse, Noah Ruddock, and William Baker, the owners of the ship the *Dispatch*, issued the following detailed instructions to the ship's captain, William Barry, before he set out on a voyage first to Africa, then to the West Indies or South Carolina, in 1725. Barry was to sail directly to Andoni, on the southeastern coast of Nigeria (about where Olaudah Equiano had first encountered Europeans) to purchase only Africans who were "healthy and strong and of a Convenient Age" and to take care that "the sailors dont abuse them." But, in case many of the slaves died anyway, Barry was also instructed to load his ship with "teeth," or ivory tusks, "seeing in that Commodity there's no Mortality to be feard." To Barry and the men who financed this voyage, the African men, women, and children on board were simply commodities to be bought and sold.

Bristol, Oct. 7th, 1725.

Capt. Wm. Barry, As the wind is inclineing to be fair you are ordered with your Men (which we allow to be 20 in Number your self included) to repair on board the Dispatch Briggtine [brigantine] of which you are Counted Commander and to loose no time but sail directly takeing the pilott with you so far as the Holmes and at his return let us be advised whether all the hands are on board and what else may be Material.

You must make the best of your Way to the Coast of Africa that is to that part of it calld Andony (without toutching or tarrying at any other place) w[h]ere you are to slave intirely, but as our Briggitine draws deep water, wee are not Inclinable you should proceed over the Barr, but rather than you Anchor as Usual in the bests and Conveniens place for safety so well as slaveing.

The Cargo of goods are of your Own ordering, and as it's very good in kind and amounts to thirteen hundred and thirty pounds eight shillings and 2 1/4 [pence] we hope twill purchase you 240 Choice slaves, besides a Quantity of teeth the latter of which are always to embrace provided they are large, seeing in that Commodity there's no Mortality to be feard. As to the slaves let your endeavours be to buy none but what's healthy and strong and of a Convenient Age—none to exceed the years of 25 or under 10 if posible, among which so many men, and stout men boys as can be had seeing such are most Valuable at the Plantations.

Let your Care be in preserving so well as in purchasing, in order to which let their provisions be well and Carefully look'd after and boild and that its given them in due season, to see the sailors dont abuse them which has often been done to the prejudice of the Voyage. So soon as you begin to slave let your knetting be fix'd breast high fore and aft and so keep 'em shackled and hand Bolted fearing their rising or leaping Overboard, to prevent which let always a constant and Carefull watch be appointed to which [you] must give the strictest Charge for the preservation of their Own Lives, so well as yours and on which the Voyage depends, which per sleeping in their Watch has often been fatall and many a good Voyage (which otherwise might have been made) entirely ruind. . . .

Be carefull of fire and in fine of all committed to your Charge, and keeping us advised by all Opportunitys of all materiall Occurrences is what imediatly offers but recommending you to the Good God Almighty's protection and wishing you a good Voyage we Remain

Your Affectionate Friends

Isaac Hobhouse

No. Ruddock

Wm. Baker

Slaves mine and wash gold as a Spanish overseer counts the nuggets. African slaves in the Americas performed a variety of tasks, from laboring in mines and on plantations to building houses and doing household work.

After a European slave-trading ship arrived on the western coast of Africa, it might take several months to purchase slaves and stock up on provisions before setting off across the Atlantic. Buyers were particular—and ruthless—about what kinds of people would make the most suitable, and thus the most valuable, slaves. Typically, they bought more

men than women and, as seen in the previous document, favored young or middle-aged people over children and the elderly. George Kingston, captain of the English ship the *Arthur*, kept a record of the enslaved men, women, and children he bought in Guinea in 1678. His journal soon turned, however, into an "Acct of what Negroes Dyd [Died] every day," as the horrible conditions on board ship took the lives of more and more Africans. Kingston's accounting is full of numbers, but he offers little other information about the people dying on his ship—not their names, where they came from, or any other details to acknowledge his common humanity with them.

Wednesday 13 February 1677. The 12th day wee Bought 3 men 3 women as your hon'rs will finde one my Books of Acc'tt and this day we Bo[ought] 14 men and 18 women very good and young negroes with some provisions for them. . . .

Sunday 17th Feby. 1677. Bo't 10 men 5 women 1 Boy and 3 girles all very likely negroes nott one of them exceedinge 30 years nor one under 14 yeares.

Monday 18th Feby 1677. This day wee Bo't 4 men and 4 women havinge noe encouridgm't to By more by Reason of shore Remissniss in Bringing us provitions Doubtinge wee should have more Negroes then wee were Likely to have provitions and soe they to take advantage that did forbarre to Bye sendinge away again severall negroes and keepinge only such as we had minde to.

Wednesday 20th Feb. 1677. This day we had Cannows [canoes] from Callabar and wee Bought 6 men 67 women and on Boye but had very Littell provitions from [for?] them. . . .

Friday 1st March 1677. This day wee Bought 13 men and 4 women very good negroes with some provitions: wee have some of our seamen sick and doubt we shall Loose some: Butt the Incouragement and hopes of not stayinge Long here is our greatest Comfortt and Trust shall bee Ready to goe from this place in three weeks tyme more our Businiss fully perfected as to our Negroes and provitions. . . .

Sattday 2 March 1677. This day wee Brought 2 men and 2 women havinge nott many Cannows one Board of us did Forbare to Buy too many expectinge to have as wee did Resolve our Choice of negroes: wee have made Choice of negroes to the Best of our skill and Judgm'tt and as likely negroes as a man should see

Yellow Will brought me off a boy slave, 3 foot 10 inches, which I was obliged to take or get nothing.

—John Newton, English slave ship captain (1751), on how he broke a pledge not to buy slaves under 4 feet tall

yett wee finde that some of them doe decay and grow Leane and some are sick they want for no thinge havinge dealy as much provition as they cann make kuse of neither doe th[ey] want for any Comfortt not suffering any man one Board to strike them.

Acct of what Negroes Dyd every day

Sunday 3 March 1677. This day wee Bought 5 men and 5 women and some provitions: aboutt 2 in the morning died one of our seamen after 5 days sickness and about 4 in the afternoon died one negro man: have 5 others sick. . . .

Fryday 8. This day wee Bought 2 men and 1 woman. . . . The 7 day aboutt four in the afternoon died one woman. This day as will appeare y're accompt wee did not purchase any Negroes Butt some provitions for negroes: wee have many sick Captives Butt take the greatest Care wee can to preserve [them].

Sattday 9, March 1677/8. This day wee Bought 8 men and 6 women very Likely Negroes with some provitions—wee had died this day one man and severall others that are sick nottwithstandinge our Care with the Docktors phisick there is nothinge wantinge to them. . . .

Tuesday 12, March 1677/8. This day wee purchased 1 man 4 women and 1 Boy with some provitions as will appeare pr Accontt and att 10 in the forenoon died one man which to our knolidge had nott been sick 12 houres.

Acc't of the Slaves mortallity rec'd out of the "John Alexander".

June 15th 1676	Day	Men	Women	Boys	Girls	
In Nevis	15		1			{ both very thin and Weake
	16		1			{ when rec'd.
	17		1			very thin when rec'd.
	19	1				
	20		1			
	21		2			
	22		2			
		1	8			

Ships of Death

After enduring a long voyage to the coast from their homes in the interior of the continent, and then often suffering a lengthy incarceration in European forts or in ships' holds, the enslaved men, women, and children had only just begun

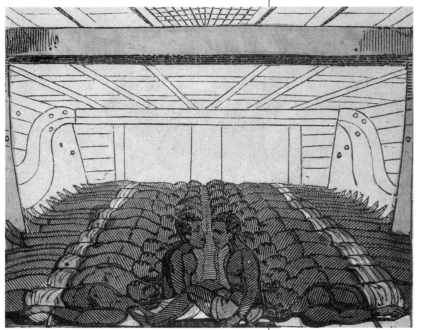

An 1826 British picture series for children does not ignore the horrors Africans endured during the passage to America.

their tortuous journey. Once a slave ship was filled with its human cargo, it began its trip across the Atlantic. The voyage itself usually took 40 to 60 days, with a typical ship carrying about 200 slaves. Olaudah Equiano recalled that conditions worsened as the days passed. When it was at all possible, it was not uncommon for people to throw themselves overboard to drown, believing that death brought a person back to his or her homeland.

The stench of the hold while we were on the coast was so intolerably loathsome that it was dangerous to remain there for any time, and some of us had been permitted to stay on the deck for the fresh air; but now that the whole ship's cargo were confined together it became absolutely pestilential. The closeness of the place and the heat of the climate, added to the number in the ship, which was so crowded that each had scarcely room to turn himself, almost suffocated us. This produced copious perspirations, so that the air soon became unfit for respiration from a variety of loathsome smells, and brought on a sickness among the slaves, of which many died, thus falling victims to the improvident avarice, as I may call it, of their purchasers. This wretched situation was again aggravated by the galling of the chains, now become insupportable, and the filth of the necessary tubs, into which the children often fell and were almost suffocated. The shrieks of the women and the groans of the dying rendered the whole a scene of horror almost inconceivable. Happily perhaps for myself I was soon reduced so low that it was thought necessary to keep me almost always on deck, and from my extreme youth I was not put in fetters. . . . One day, when we had a smooth sea and moderate wind, two of my wearied countrymen who were chained together (I was near them at the time), preferring death to such a life of misery, somehow made through the nettings and jumped into the sea: immediately another dejected fellow, who on account of his illness was suffered to be out of irons, also followed their example; and I believe many more would very soon have done the same if they had not been prevented by the ship's crew.

An Acc'tt of the Mortallity of Slaves aboord the Shipp "James".[32]

1675	Day	Men	Women	Boys	Girls	
Abbenee [September]	6	1				Departed this Life suddenly.
Temenn October	28			1		Departed this life of Convulsion Fitts
Agga December	20	1				Departed this life of a feavour
Cape Corso January 1675/6	20	1				Rec'd from Wyemba thin and Consumed to Nothing and soe dyed
Ditto	26		1			Rec'd from Wyemba very thin and wasted to Nothing and soe dyed
Suckingdee February 1675/6	8	1				Rec'd from Wyemba very thin and dropsicall and soe departed this life.
Thwort of Butteren [33]	23		1			bought to Windward and departed this life of a Consumption and Wormes.

For Sale

After arriving in the Americas, enslaved Africans were sold either at a public auction in a port town or through advertisements in local newspapers. Those who were born into slavery on plantations were not necessarily spared the experience of being brought to auction, however, since many were resold later in life. Mary Prince was born into slavery in Bermuda in the last years of the 18th century. Until she was 12 years old, she lived on a plantation there with her mother and younger siblings, but when her owner died Mary and her family were taken to town to be sold. The following passage, from Mary's own account—the first slave narrative written by a woman—describes how she and her mother and sister were brought to an auction, where they were inspected like "dumb beasts" and ultimately sold to different buyers. Here, Mary eloquently describes the horror of the auction, the terror of being separated from her family, and, most of all, her sense of helplessness in the face of a wholly brutalizing process.

Our mother, weeping as she went, called me away with the children Hannah and Dinah, and we took the road that led to Hamble Town, which we reached about four o'clock in the afternoon. We

Advertisements of slaves for sale in South Carolina. The one on top claims that a new shipment of Africans has just arrived from the "rice coast," important information for plantation owners cultivating rice and depending on workers who knew how to harvest it.

followed my mother to the market-place, where she placed us in a row against a large house, with our backs to the wall and our arms folded across our breasts. I, as the eldest, stood first, Hannah next to me, then Dinah; and our mother stood beside, crying over us. My heart throbbed with grief and terror so violently, that I pressed my hands quite tightly across my breast, but I could not keep it still, and it continued to leap as though it would burst out of my body. But who cared for that? Did one of the many by-standers, who were looking at us so carelessly, think of the pain that wrung the hearts of the negro woman and her young ones? No, no! . . . At length the vendue master, who was to offer us for sale like sheep or cattle, arrived, and asked my mother which was the eldest. She said nothing, but pointed to me. He took me by the hand, and led me out to the middle of the street, and, turning me slowly round, exposed me to the view of those who attended the vendue. I was soon surrounded by strange men, who examined and handled me in the same manner that a butcher would a calf or a lamb he was about to purchase, and who talked about my shape and size in like words—as if I could no more understand their meaning than the dumb beasts. I was then put up to sale. The bidding commenced at a few pounds, and gradually rose to fifty-seven, when I was knocked down to the highest bidder; and the people who stood by said that I had fetched a great sum for so young a slave.

I then saw my sisters led forth, and sold to different owners; so that we had not the sad satisfaction of being partners in bondage. When the sale was over, my mother hugged and kissed us, and mourned over us, begging of us to keep up a good heart, and do our duty to our new masters. It was a sad parting; one went one way, one another, and our poor mammy went home with nothing.

Africans' New Worlds

In the Americas, Africans experienced their own New World. In the British colonies, the slave populations were the largest in the Caribbean, on Barbados and Jamaica. On the North American mainland, Virginia, Maryland, and South Carolina had the greatest numbers of Africans. In Virginia, the percentage of blacks in the population grew from under

10 percent in 1650 to almost 50 percent in 1750. It was slave labor that made Virginia's tremendous prosperity possible as the colony focused its energy on the cultivation of a single crop: tobacco. Before turning to tobacco, Virginia had floundered. But, this phenomenal cash crop brought tremendous prosperity to the region. Between 1619 and 1700, production of tobacco in the British colonies rose from annual exports of just 20,000 pounds to 38 million pounds. Most of this tobacco was grown in the Chesapeake Bay area, the majority of it by Africans working under conditions of permanent servitude.

Hugh Jones, an Englishman brought to Virginia to teach at the College of William and Mary, described slave life as he saw it there in the 1720s. Jones's account deals primarily with Africans involved in field labor on large plantations, but Africans did many different kinds of work in a variety of settings.

The Negroes live in small cottages called quarters, in about six in a gang, under the direction of an overseer or bailiff; who takes care that they tend such land as the owner allots and orders, upon which they raise hogs and cattle, and plant Indian corn (or maize) and tobacco for the use of their master; out of which the overseer has a dividend (or share) in proportion to the number of hands including himself; this with several privileges is his salary, and is an ample recompence for his pains, and encouragement of his industrious care, as to the labor, health, and provision of the Negroes.

The Negroes are very numerous, some gentlemen having hundreds of them of all sorts, to whom they bring great profit; for the sake of which they are obliged to keep them well, and not overwork, starve, or famish them, besides other inducements to favor them; which is done in a great degree, to such especially that are laborious, careful, and honest; though indeed some masters careless of their own interest or reputation, are too cruel and negligent.

The Negroes are not only encreased by fresh supplies from Africa and the West Indian Islands, but also are very prolifick among themselves; and they that are born here talk good English, and affect our language, habits, and customs; and though they be naturally of a barbarous and cruel temper, yet are they kept under by severe discipline upon occasion, and by good laws are prevented from running away, injuring the English, or neglecting their business.

Because of the torture of bringing children into a life of perpetual slavery, and the prospect of being separated from them by being sold, many African men and women tried to avoid pregnancy by abstaining from sex. Rates of fertility were incredibly low, especially among enslaved people brought directly from Africa, and those populations never grew through what social scientists call "natural increase." Instead, slave populations grew only through the continued importation of new slaves. Reduced sexual activity was not the only cause of low fertility. First, many more African men than women were enslaved (probably three men for every woman). Second, both men and women were typically weak and in poor health due to the harshness of the middle passage and the terrible conditions under which they labored. Depression probably also played a role. And fourth, some African women (as well as enslaved Native American women and, for that matter, Euroamerican women) used herbal abortifacients, or abortion-inducing herbs, to end pregnancies. Abortion rates, like the many suicides committed on slave ships by Africans throwing themselves into the water to drown, were affected by many Africans' religious conviction that at death a soul returns to its homeland. Many potential parents no doubt believed that sending a soul to a peaceful afterlife in Africa was far preferable to the miseries of slavery in the Americas. At the end of the 17th century, the Dutch artist and naturalist Maria Sibylla Merian, who lived in Suriname for two years, recorded some local uses of a natural abortifacient plant called peacock flower:

"Its seeds are used by women who are in childbirth in order to promote labor quickly. Indians, who are not well treated in their servitude by the Dutch, use it to abort their children so that they will not become slaves like them. The black slaves from Guinea and Angola must be treated benignly, otherwise they will produce no children at all in their state of slavery. Nor do they have any. Indeed, they even kill themselves on account of the harsh treatment to which they are ordinarily subject. For they feel that they will be born again with their friends in a free state in their own country, so they instructed me out of their own mouths."

*They import so many Negros
hither that I fear this Colony
[Virginia] will some time or other
be confirmed by the Name of
New Guinea.*

—William Byrd II (1736)

*The cartouche on a 1751 map
of Maryland and Virginia
celebrates the Chesapeake's
profitable tobacco trade.
African slaves bring barrels of
cured tobacco leaves to port,
while white plantation owners
negotiate the prices.*

Their work (or chimerical hard slavery) is not very laborious; their greatest hardship consisting in that they and their posterity are not at their own liberty or disposal, but are the property of their owners; and when they are free, they know not how to provide so well for themselves generally; neither did they live so plentifully nor (many of them) so easily in their own country, where they are made slaves to one another, or taken captive by their enemies. . . .

Several of them are taught to be sawyers, carpenters, smiths, coopers, etc., and though for the most part they be none of the aptest or nicest; yet they are by nature cut out for hard labour and fatigue, and will perform tolerably well; though they fall much short of an Indain, that has learned and seen the same things; and those Negroes make the best servants, that have been slaves in their own country, for they that have been kings and great men are generally lazy, haughty, and obstinate; whereas the others are sharper, better humored, and more laborious. . . .

As for baptizing Indians and Negroes, several of the people disapprove of it; because they say it often makes them proud, and not so good servants: But these, and such objections, are easily refuted, if the persons be sensible, good, and understand English, and have been taught (or are willing to learn) the principles of Christianity, and if they be kept to the observance of it afterwards; for Christianity encourages and orders them to be more humble and better servants, and not worse, than when they were heathens.

But as for the children of Negroes and Indians, that are to live among Christians, undoubtedly they ought all to be baptized; since it is not out of the power of their masters to take care that they have a Christian education, learn their prayers and catechism, and go to church, and not accustom themselves to lie, swear and steal, though such (as the poorer sort in England) be not taught to read and write; which as yet has been found to be dangerous upon several political accounts, especially self-preservation.

In Bermuda, Mary Prince worked in fields as an agricultural-ist, but she rarely worked on large plantations. Instead, she worked (and usually lived) in the house of her owner, where she did domestic work. Prince, like all enslaved African women, was vulnerable to sexual exploitation—the men who owned or supervised women slaves could often rape, abuse, or even murder them with impunity. In her autobiog-raphy, Prince reports many such incidents, as did other writ-ers. The slave owners' methods of disciplining their enslaved laborers ranged from whipping to amputation, and few were spared witnessing such tortures, if not enduring them. Prince suffered unendurable abuse at the hands of her owner, "Mr. D—," who repeatedly had her stripped naked and hung by her wrists while he whipped her. In fact, Mr. D beat not only his slaves but his daughter as well. In this passage, Prince intervenes on the daughter's behalf, only to be punished. Prince, however, attempts to curb Mr. D's aggression by reminding him that they are no longer on Turk's Island, a remote place where abuse of slaves was entirely unchecked and where they had recently been living.

I was several years the slave of Mr. D—. . . . Here I worked in the grounds. My work was planting and hoeing sweet-potatoes, Indian corn, plaintains, bananas, cabbages, pumpkins, onions, &c. I did all the household work, and attended upon a horse and cow besides, —going also upon all errands. I had to curry the horse—to clean and feed him—and sometimes to ride him a little. I had more than enough to do —but still it was not so very bad as Turk's Island.

My old master often got drunk, and then he would get in a fury with his daughter, and beat her till she was not fit to be seen. I remember on one occasion, I had gone to fetch water, and when I was coming up the hill I heard a great screaming; I ran as fast as I could to the house, put down the water, and went into the cham-ber, where I found my master beating Miss D— dreadfully. I strove with all my strength to get her away from him; for she was all black and blue with bruises. He had beat her with his fist, and almost killed her. The people gave me credit for getting her away. He turned round and began to lick me. Then I said, "Sir, this is not Turk's Island." I can't repeat his answer, the words were too wicked—too bad to say. He wanted to treat me the same in Bermuda as he had done in Turk's Island.

He had an ugly fashion of stripping himself quite naked and ordering me then to wash him in a tub of water. This was worse to

This 18th-century scene from a South Carolina rice plantation depicts a slave dancing while a crowd watches. A banjo player and drummer provide the music. In many communities in America, Africans were able to maintain the traditions of their homelands.

me than all the licks. Sometimes when he called me to wash him I would not come, my eyes were so full of shame. He would then come to beat me. One time I had plates and knives in my hand, and I dropped both plates and knives, and some of the plates were broken. He struck me so severely for this, that at last I defended myself, for I thought it was high time to do so. I then told him I would not live longer with him, for he was a very indecent man — very spiteful, and too indecent; with no shame for his servants, no shame for his own flesh. So I went away to a neighboring house and sat down and cried till the next morning, when I went home again, not knowing what else to do.

Two Views

Opposition to the African slave trade grew in England over the course of the 18th century, in large part due to the eloquent and powerful writings of former slaves like Olaudah Equiano, but also because of antislavery tracts by former slave traders like John Newton, who wrote in 1780, "I hope it will always be a subject of humiliating reflection to me, that I was once an active instrument in a business at which my heart

now shudders." As the 18th century progressed, opposition to slavery was also influenced by the growth of ideas about freedom, liberty, and independence that would eventually lead to the American Revolution. Occasionally, however, these same ideas were used instead to defend the slave trade, as this passage from the *London Magazine* in 1740 illustrates.

The Inhabitants of Guinea are indeed in a most deplorable State of Slavery, under the arbitrary Powers of their Princes both as to Life and Property. In the several Subordinations to them, every great Man is absolute lord of his immediate Dependents. And lower still; every Master of a Family is Proprietor of his Wives, Children, and Servants; and may at his Pleasure consign them to Death, or a better Market. No doubt such a state is contrary to Nature and Reason, since every human Creature hath an absolute Right to Liberty. But are not all arbitrary Governments, as well in Europe, as Africa, equally repugnant to that great Law of Nature? And yet it is not in our Power to cure the universal Evil, and set all the Kingdoms of the Earth free from the Domination of Tyrants. . . .

All that can be done in such a Case is, to communicate as much Liberty, and Happiness, as such circumstances will admit, and the People will consent to it: And this is certainly [accomplished] by the Guinea Trade. For, by purchasing, or rather ransoming the Negroes from their national Tyrants, and transplanting them under the benign Influences of the Law, and Gospel, they are advanced to much greater Degrees of Felicity, tho' not to absolute Liberty.

That this is truly the Case cannot be doubted by any one acquainted with the Constitution of our Colonies, where the Negroes are governed by Laws, and suffer much less Punishment in Proportion to their Crimes, than the People in other Countries more refined in the Arts of Wickedness. . . .

Mary Prince offered a passionate rebuttal to those who advocated the position of the writer for the *London Magazine*.

I am often very much vexed, and I feel great sorrow when I hear some people in this country say, that the slaves do not need better usage, and do not want to be free. They believe the foreign people, who deceive them, and say slaves are happy. I say, Not so. How can slaves be happy when they have the halter round their neck and the whip upon their back? and are disgraced and thought no more of than beasts?—and are separated from their

Whereas the frequent meeting of considerable numbers of negroe slaves under pretence of feasts and burialls is judged of dangerous consequence; for prevention whereof for the future, Bee it enacted by the kings most excellent majestie by and with the consent of the generall assembly, and it is hereby enacted by the authority aforesaid, that from and after the publication of this law, it shall not be lawfull for any negroe or other slave to carry or arme himselfe with any club, staffe, gunn, sword or any other weapon of defence or offence, nor to goe to [or] depart from of his masters ground without a certificate from him as aforesaid shalbe sent to the next constable, who is hereby enjoyned and required to give the said negroe twenty lashes on his bare back well layd on, and soe sent home to his said master, mistris or overseer. And it is further enacted by the authority aforesaid that if any negroe or other slave shall presume to lift up his hand in opposition against any christian, shall for every such offence, upon due proofe made thereof by the oath of the party before a magistrate, have and receive thirty lashes on his bare back well laid on. And it is hereby further enacted by the authority aforesaid that if any negroe or other slave shall absent himself from his masters service and lye hid and lurking in obscure places, comitting injuries to the inhabitants, and shall resist any person or persons that shalby any lawfull authority be imployed to apprehend and take the said negroe, that then in case of such resistance, it shalbe lawfull for such person or persons to kill the said negroe or slave soe lying out and resisting. . . .

—Virginia Statutes (1680)

mothers, and husbands, and children, and sisters, just as cattle are sold and separated? Is it happiness for a driver in the field to take down his wife or sister or child, and strip them, and whip them in such a disgraceful manner? . . . [The English in the West Indies] tie up slaves like hogs—moor them up like cattle, and they lick them, so as hogs, or cattle, or horses were never flogged;—and yet they come home and say, and make some good people believe, that slaves don't want to get out of slavery. But they put a cloak about the truth. It is not so. All slaves want to be free—to be free is very sweet. . . . I have been a slave myself—I know what slaves feel—I can tell by myself what other slaves feel, and by what they have told me. The man that says slaves be quite happy in slavery—that they don't want to be free—that man is either ignorant or a lying person.

Runaways and Rebels

Blacks in British North America resisted slavery in many different ways: they formed sustaining friendships and built loving families; they used what little free time they had to enjoy the community of friends and relatives during dances and rituals and ceremonies; they composed and sang songs and created quilts and baskets and engaged in other expressive craft forms; they undermined their masters' goals by slowing down their labor or deliberately subverting tasks. They even staged insurrections, resorting to whatever means were available to escape the misery of slavery. In June 1729, the lieutenant governor of Virginia, William Gooch, wrote to the colony's board of trade to alert them to one such rebellion.

My Lords:
Sometime after my last a number of Negroes, about fifteen, belonging to a new Plantation on the head of James River formed a Design to withdraw from their master and to fix themselves in the fastnesses of the neighboring Mountains. They had found means to get into their possession some Arms & Ammunition, and they took along with them some Povsions, their Cloaths, bedding and working Tools; but the Gentlemen to whom they belonged with a party of Men made such diligent pursuit after them, that he soon found them out in their new Settlement, a very obscure place among the Mountains, where they had already begun to clear the ground, and obliged them after exchanging a shot or two by which one of the Slaves was wounded, to surrender and return

back, and so prevented for this time a design which might have proved as dangerous to this Country, as is that of the Negroes in the Mountains of Jamaica to the Inhabitants of that Island. Tho' this attempt has happily been defeated, it ought nevertheless to awaken us into some effectual measures for preventing the like hereafter, it being certain that a very small number of Negroes once settled in those Parts, would very soon be encreas'd by the Accession of other Runaways and prove dangerous Neighbors to our frontier Inhabitants. To prevent this and many other Mischiefs I am training and exercising the Militia in the several counties as the best means to deter our Slaves from endeavoring to make their Escape, and to suppress them if they should.

Chapter Seven

Planting New England

J ohn Sassamon, a Massachusett Algonquian Indian, saw it all. When he was born, in the late 1620s, English colonists had only just arrived in the land they called New England. Sassamon must have met English men and women when he was a young child. The first sustained English settlement near his home began in 1620, when a group of separatists from the Church of England founded Plymouth Colony. Ten years after these Plymouth "pilgrims" arrived, another group of colonists, mainly Protestants calling themselves Puritans, established the nearby Massachusetts Bay Colony. Between 1630 and 1660, a great migration of English men and women followed, some 20,000 in all, fleeing crowded conditions in England and hoping to establish religious sanctuary in America.

Over the course of his lifetime, Sassamon witnessed a rapid growth of English settlers and, simultaneously, a precipitous decline in the native Algonquian population. Even before the *Mayflower* set sail for the New World, European contagions from earlier explorations had affected the native Algonquian Indian population. A great plague in 1616–18 took thousands of lives among the coastal Algonquians. Before that epidemic, the native population of the area was probably between 72,000 and 90,000, but as much as 90 percent of the population may have died in that and succeeding epidemics. The English settlers, who always sought signs of God's providence in the natural world, took the plague of 1616–18 as a sign that New England had been divinely depopulated to make room for them. The Indians sought divine interpretation for these events as well, some no doubt fearing that their gods, or manitous, had abandoned them.

John Sassamon was one of only a few Algonquians living near the English to survive a devastating smallpox epidemic in 1633; his parents were not so lucky. Orphaned, John grew up in the town of Dorchester, Massachusetts, probably as a servant in an English house. Of such servants one Puritan wrote, "Divers of the Indians Children,

This 1590 Théodore de Bry etching of life in a Native American village pays careful attention to the Indians' planting and gardening techniques. The village appears to be a permanent settlement, but after a dozen years or so the villagers will move, largely because of depleted soil nutrients and insect problems.

Designed in 1629, the seal of the Massachusetts Bay Colony depicts an American Indian at the center, calling to the Puritans to "come over and help us." The Puritans sought to convert the Indians to Christianity, and also to acquire their land.

The hand of God fell heavily upon them, with such a mortall stroake, that they died in heapes, as they lay in their houses; and the living, that were unable to shift for themselves, would runne away and let them dy, and let there Carkases ly above the ground without buriall. For in a place where many inhabited, there hath been but one left a live, to tell what became of the rest, the livinge being (as it seems) not able to bury the dead, they were left for Crowes, Kites and vermin to pray [prey] upon. And the bones and skulls upon the severall places of their habitations, made such a spectacle after my comming into those parts, that as I travailed in that Forrest, nere the Massachussets, it seemd to mee a new found Golgatha.

—Thomas Morton, 1637, on Algonquians as plague victims

Boyes and Girles we have received into our houses, who are long since civilized, and in subjection to us." These children, he proudly announced, "can speak our language familiarly; divers of whom can read English, and begin to understand in their measure, the grounds of Christian Religion." Sassamon, too, learned English and even was able to read and write, in a time when many English men and women remained illiterate.

From the English, Sassamon also learned to use a gun. In 1637 he fought alongside the colonists in a war against the Pequot Indians in Connecticut. When one Pequot saw Sassamon dressed "in English clothes, and a gun in his hand," he called out to him, "What are you, an Indian or an Englishman?" Sassamon was by birth an Indian, but he had lived much of his life among the English and had converted to their religion. By way of answering the Pequot's question, Sassamon called out, "Come hither, and I will tell you." When the Pequot approached, Sassamon shot him dead. His loyalties clearly lay with the English.

After the war against the Pequots, Sassamon returned to Dorchester, where he soon began working as a translator and interpreter for a Puritan minister named John Eliot. Eliot wanted to teach more Algonquians to read and write and become Christians, so Sassamon helped him learn Massachusett, the Algonquian dialect he spoke. Together, Sassamon and Eliot translated the entire Bible into Massachusett. To further his preparation for the ministry, in 1653 Sassamon briefly attended Harvard College. Soon he became a minister, preaching to a town of converted Christian Indians.

More than any other single colonial venture in British North America, the English settlement of New England was religiously inspired, but the fervor that drove the venture had more to do with maintaining the piety of the colonists than with converting the natives to Christianity. The Puritans announced time and again that preaching to the Indians was among their chief goals, but in reality, Puritan ministers were slow to take an interest in converting the Algonquians. When they did make the effort, however, these ministers made a point of distinguishing themselves from the French and Spanish missionaries, who converted the Indians simply by baptizing them. The English missionaries first attempted to teach the Indians to read, that they might encounter God directly through the Bible.

John Sassamon was the key to the Puritans' missionary project. Like Malinalli, who translated and interpreted for Cortés, John Sassamon became a valued interpreter. Like her, he probably suffered for occupying a treacherous position between two worlds—one Indian, the other English. As the Puritans' efforts to convert the Indians foundered, so did Sassamon's own position. Making the Indians good Christians, it seemed, competed with the settlers' designs for Indian lands. Perhaps more powerfully, the Puritans' brand of proselytizing competed with the Algonquians' own desire for cultural autonomy.

In the 1660s and 1670s, Sassamon attempted to convert a powerful Wampanoag Indian leader named Metacom, whom the English called Philip, to Christianity. Sassamon failed to convert Metacom, but he did find out that Philip was planning a war against the English. In December 1675, Sassamon traveled to Plymouth to tell the English governor of Philip's plans, but the governor didn't believe him. Within a few weeks, Sassamon's body was found under the ice in a nearby pond. The English, suspecting Philip had had Sassamon killed for his betrayal, tried and executed three of Philip's chief counselors the following June. In a matter of days, war broke out. A little more than a half century after the *Mayflower* docked in Plymouth Bay, a confederation of local Indians—increasingly frustrated by English incursions on their land and culture—waged war on the English settlers in a desperate attempt to oust them from New England. John Sassamon's death, many English and Algonquians alike believed, was the cause of it all.

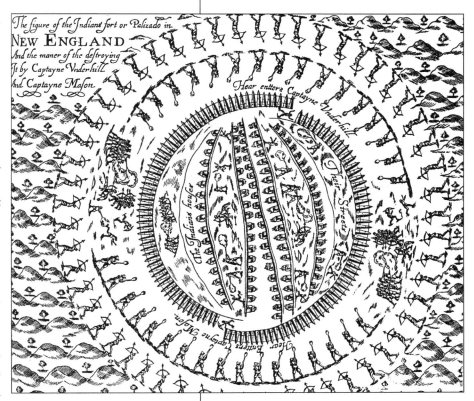

This illustration of the 1637 attack on the Pequot Indians of Connecticut appeared in John Underhill's Newes from America. The Pequot were a dominant tribe in 17th-century New England. British colonists and their Mohegan and Narragansett allies attacked the main Pequot village at night. Several hundred defenders, including women and children, were burned alive. By the end of the Pequot War, the tribe was nearly wiped out.

Metacom's Rebellion

When war erupted in June 1675 between the English and the Indians in New England, the English settlers had been taking more and more Indian land, often in defiance of even their own laws, and those of the Indians who were non-Christian had grown increasingly resentful of the colonists' efforts to

The year 1676 was a bloody one for England's colonies. In New England, the Algonquian uprising led by Metacom (King Philip) caused the English to abandon over half their settlements, and took the lives of more than one in ten colonists. In Virginia, the powerful Susquehannocks raided frontier settlements in a conflict that came to be called Bacon's Rebellion. And in Barbados, enslaved Africans staged a revolt. Coincidence? The colonial authorities did not think so. The governor of Virginia was convinced that Indians from New England had conspired with their neighbors to the south. "The infection of the Indianes in New-England," he complained, "has dilated it selfe to the Merilanders and the Northern parts of Virginia." Meanwhile, in Boston, Nathaniel Saltonstall believed that Barbados and New England had "tasted of the same Cup"; to drive home his point, Saltonstall even published accounts of the two uprisings bound together in the same book. And, when New Englanders tried to sell captured Indians to slave masters in Barbados, that government turned the ships away at port: its legislature had already passed a law barring the purchase of any Indians from New England, they "being thought a people of too subtle, bloody and dangerous inclination to be and remain here."

Were King Philip's War, Bacon's Rebellion, and the Barbadian slave revolt related? Yes and no. There was not, as many English men and women feared, a grand conspiracy of Africans and Native Americans behind the events of 1676, but the revolts were related. In New England and Virginia, the English colonists had become more and more ruthless in acquiring Indian lands by any means necessary, and their attacks on Indian settlements were bound to be met with resistance. In Barbados, where Africans had begun to outnumber English residents by 1660, the conditions of slavery were even more brutal and torturous than elsewhere.

Just four years after the calamitous events of 1676, Pueblo Indians in New Mexico staged their own revolt, this time against an altogether different colonizing power, Spain. In a brilliantly coordinated uprising, 17,000 Pueblo Indians—living in more than two dozen towns spread out over several hundred miles and speaking six different languages—all revolted on a single day, August 10. The rebels attacked Spanish soldiers and missionaries, destroyed Spanish buildings, and laid waste to Spanish crops, successfully forcing the Spanish to abandon their settlement of New Mexico.

convert them. Metacom, the leader of the Algonquian Wampanoag Indians, was at the center of the conflict later called King Philip's War, in which the Wampanoag, Nipmuck, and Narragansett Indians all fought against the English. Many Indians, however, fought alongside the colonists, including converted Indians and the Mohegan and Pequot tribes. Just a few days after the outbreak of war, Metacom spoke with John Easton, the deputy governor of Rhode Island, and explained to him the many grievances against the English that had led him to war.

[Metacom and his counselors said] that thay had a great fear to have ani of ther indians should be Caled or forsed to be Christian indians. thay saied that such wer in everi thing more mischivous, only disemblers, and then the English made them not subject to ther kings, and by ther lying to rong their kings. we knew it to be true. . . . thay saied thay had bine the first in doing good to the English, and the English the first in doing rong, saied when the English first Came their kings father was as a great man and the English as a litell Child, he Constraened other indians from ronging the English and gave them Coren and shewed them how to plant and was free to do them ani good and had let them have a 100 times more land, then now the king had for his own peopell. . . . another greavanc was if 20 of there onest indians testefied that a Englishman had dun them wrong, it was as nothing, and if but one of ther worst indians testefied against ani indian or ther king when it plesed the English that was sufitiant. a nother grivanc was when ther kings sold land the English wold say it was more than thay agred to and a writing must be prove against all them, and sum of ther kings had dun rong to sell so much he left his peopell none and sum being given to drunknes the English made them drunk and then cheted them in bargens. . . . a nother grivanc the English Catell and horses still incresed that when thay removed 30 mill from wher English had anithing to do, thay Could not kepe ther coren from being spoyled, thay never being iused to fence, and thoft [thought] when the English boft [bought] land of them that thay wold have kept ther Catell upone ther owne land. a nother grevanc the English wear so eger to sell the indians lickers that most of the indians spent all in drunknes and then ravened uponde the sober indians and thay did belive often did hurt the English Catell, and ther kings Could not prevent it.

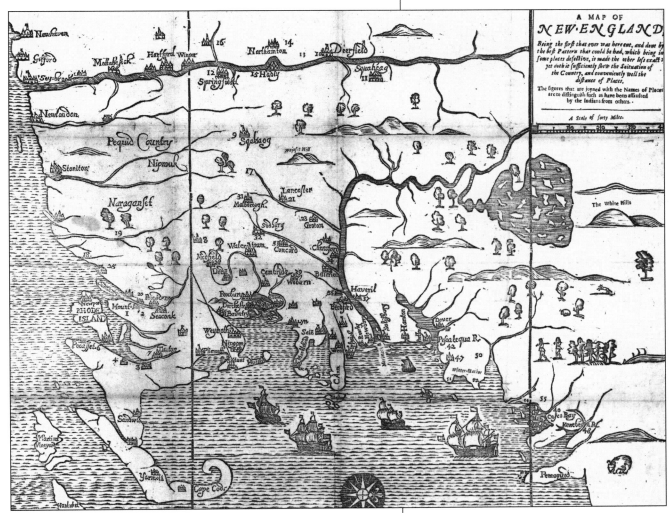

A 1676 map of New England, with Boston situated in the bay in the center, a few inches above the curling peninsula labeled Cape Cod. Many Massachusetts towns were destroyed by the Indians during King Philip's War.

Among the English towns destroyed in King Philip's War was Lancaster, Massachusetts, where Mary Rowlandson, the minister's wife, was taken captive. She lived among the Indians for over three months before she was released. When she returned home, she wrote an account of her captivity that was later published and became one of America's first bestsellers. Here she describes the Indian attack on her town.

On the tenth of February 1675 [1676], came the Indians with great numbers upon Lancaster: Their first coming was about sunrising; hearing the noise of some guns, we looked out; several houses were burning, and the smoke ascending to heaven. There were five persons taken in one house, the father, and the mother, and a sucking child, they knocked on the head; the other two they took and carried away alive. There were two others, who being

A
NARRATIVE
OF THE
CAPTIVITY, SUFFERINGS AND REMOVES
OF
Mrs. *Mary Rowlandſon,*

Who was taken Priſoner by the INDIANS with ſeveral others, and treated in the moſt barbarous and cruel Manner by thoſe vile Savages : With many other remarkable Events during her TRAVELS.

Written by her own Hand, for her private Uſe, and now made public at the earneſt Deſire of ſome Friends, and for the Benefit of the afflicted.

BOSTON

Printed and Sold at JOHN BOYLE'S Printing-Office, next Door to the *Three Doves* in Marlborough-Street. 1773.

Mary Rowlandson's account of her "captivity and restoration" was one of the first best-sellers in America. She claims on the title page that this account was originally written for her "private life" but has been presented to the public in the hope that it may benefit the "afflicted," or those who have also endured God's trials.

out of their garrison upon some occasion were set upon; one was knocked on the head, the other escaped: another there was who running along was shot and wounded, and fell down; he begged of them his life, promising them money (as they told me) but they would not hearken to him but knocked him in the head, and stripped him naked, and split open his bowels. . . .

At length they came and beset our own house, and quickly it was the dolefullest day that ever mine eyes saw. The house stood upon the edge of a hill; some of the Indians got behind the hill, others into the barn, and others behind any thing that could shelter them; from all which places they shot against the house, so that the bullets seemed to fly like hail; and quickly they wounded one man among us, then another, and then a third. About two hours (according to my observations, in that amazing time) they had been about the house before they prevailed to fire it. . . . Now is the dreadful hour come, that I have often heard of (in time of war, as it was in the case of others) but now mine eyes see it. Some in our house were fighting for their lives, others wallowing in their blood, the house on fire over our heads, and the bloody heathen ready to knock us on the head, if we stirred out. Now might we hear mothers and children crying out for themselves, and one another, Lord, What shall we do? Then I took my children (and one of my sisters, hers) to go forth and leave the house; but as soon as we came to the door and appeared, the Indians shot so thick that the bullets rattled against the house, as if one had taken a handful of stones and threw them, so that we were fain to give back. We had six stout dogs belonging to our garrison, but none of them would stir, though another time, if any Indian had come to the door, they were ready to fly upon him and tear him down. The Lord hereby would make us the more to acknowledge his hand, and to see that our help is always in him. But out we must go, the fire increasing, and coming along behind us, roaring and the Indians gaping before us with their guns, spears, and hatchets to devour us. No sooner were we out of the house, but my brother-in-law (being before wounded, in defending the house, in or near the throat) fell down dead whereat the Indians scornfully shouted and holloed, and were presently upon him, stripping off his clothes, the bullets flying thick, one went through my side and the same (as would seem) through the bowels and hand of my dear child in my arms. One of my elder sister's children, named William, had then his leg broken, which the Indians perceiving, they knocked him on the head. Thus we were butchered by those merciless heathen, standing amazed, with the blood running down to our heels.

While King Philip's War raged, the colonial governments decided that even the Christianized Indians could not be trusted. As a result, hundreds of converted Indians were confined for the duration of the war on Deer Island in Boston Harbor, where at least half died over the winter of 1675–76 from starvation and exposure. Throughout the war, captured enemy Indians (and no doubt many Christianized ones who were never involved in the war), as well as Indians who had voluntarily submitted themselves to the English were sold into slavery, many being shipped to islands in the Caribbean. John Eliot [minister of Roxbury, Mass.] attempted to halt the sale of Indians into slavery, employing the arguments that Bartolomé de Las Casas had made before the king of Spain at a famous debate in Valladolid, Spain, over a century earlier. Eliot's petition, addressed to the governor and council of Massachusetts Bay, went entirely ignored.

Petition

That the terror of selling away such Indians, unto the Ilands for perpetual slaves, who shall yeild up themselves to your mercy, is like to be an effectual plongation [prolongation] of the warre & such an exaspation of them, as may produce, we know not what evil consequences, upon all the land. Christ hath saide, blessed are the mercyfull, for thei shall obteine mercy. this usage of them is worse than death. to put to death men that have deserved to dy, is an ordinance of God, & a blessing is promised to it. it may be done in Faith. the designe of Christ in these last dayes, is not to exstirpate nations, but to gospelize them. he will spread the gospel round the world about Revelations 11: 15. the kingdoms of the world are become the kingdoms of the Lord & of his Christ. his Sovaigne hand, & grace hath brought the gospel into these dark places of the earth. when we came, we declared to the world, & it is recorded, yea we are ingaged by or letters Patent to the Kings Majesty, that the indeavour of the Indinas conversion, not theire exstirpation, was one great end of our enterprize, in coming to these ends of the earth. The Lord hath so succeeded that work, as that (by his grace) they have the holy Scriptures as sundry of themselves able to teach theire countrymen, the good knowledg of God. The light of the gospel is risen among those that sat in darknesse, & in the region of the shadow of death. And however some of them have refused to receive the gospel, & now are incensed in theire spirits unto a warre against the English: yet by that good pmise [promise] . . . I doubt not but the meaning of

After several months as a captive, Mary Rowlandson was eventually ransomed and returned to English society. But many English captives, especially those taken as children, never returned, even when they had the opportunity. Perhaps more than half the European colonists taken captive by Indians became fully adopted into their new communities and chose to remain there. No doubt these "white Indians" (many of whom were women) found Native American life appealing, in part because of its different ideas about the roles of men and women. Eunice Williams, for example, was removed from her home in Deerfield, Massachusetts, in 1704, when she was just seven years old. Eunice was taken to Canada, where she was adopted into a Mohawk family near Montreal. She soon forgot how to speak English and eventually married a Mohawk man. Eunice's father, a prominent Puritan minister, tried for years to secure her "release," even meeting with her on several occasions, but she had no desire to return. Though she and her husband (and later her children) visited her original family at Deerfield, Eunice, like many other "captives," chose deliberately to live among the Indians instead.

Christ is, to open a dore for the free passage of the gospel among ym, & that the Lord wil fulfill that word yet have I set my king, my annoynted, on my holy hill of Syon, though some rage at it. My humble request is, that you would follow Christ his designe, in this matter, to pmote [promote] the free passage of Religion among them, & not to destroy them. To send them away fro the light of the gospel, wch Christ hath graiously given them, uto a place, a state, a way of perpetual darknesse, to the eternal ruine of theire soules, is (as I apprehend) to act contrary to the mind of Christ. Gods command is, that we should inlarge the kingdom of Jesus Christ, Esay 54.2. enlarge the place of thy tent. it seemeth to me, that to sell them away for slaves, is to hinder the inlargment of his kingdom. how can a Christian soule yeild to act, in casting away theire soules, for wm, christ hath, wth an eminent hand provided an offer of the gospel to sell soules for mony seemeth to me a dangerous merchandize. if thei deserve to dy, it is far better to be put to death, under godly governors, who will take religious care, that meanes may be used, that thei may dy penitently. to sell them away fro all meanes of grace, wn Christ hath provided meanes of grace for them, is the way for us to be active in the destroying their soules, when we are highly obliged to seeke theire convsion, & salvation, & have opportunity in our hands so to doe. deut 23. 15-166, a fugitive servant from a pagan Master, might not be delivered to his master, but be kept in Israel for the good of his soule, how much lesse lawfull is it to sell away, soules from under the light of the gospell, into a condition, where theire soules will be utterly lost, so far as appeareth unto man. all men (of reading) condemne the Spaniard for cruelty, upon this poynt, in destroying men & depopulating the land. the Country is large enough, here is land enough for them & us too. p 14. 26. in the multitude of people is the kings honor. it will be much to the glory of Christ, to have many brought in to worship his great name.

I beseech the honord Council to pardon my boldnesse, & let the case of Conscience be discussed orderly, before the thing be acted, cover my weaknesse, & weigh the reason & religion that laboreth in this great case of Conscience.

"John Eliot"

John Eliot was not alone in sending petitions to the Massachusetts government during the war. Here, William Nahaton, a Christian Indian who served the English during the war, pleads for the release of a relative being sold into slavery.

To the honored counsel now siting at boston the humble petition of william ahaton hee humbly sheweth

I have seing a woman taken by the mohegins and now brought to boston which woman although she did belong to phillip his Company yet shee is a kinn to me and all so to john huntar as severall of the indians of punkapoag do know[.] my humble and right request there fore to the Renowned Counsel is that if it may stand with there plesure and with out futur inconvenience her Life may be spared and her Liberty granted under such conditions as the honored Counsel see most fit: shee being a woman whatever her mind hath been it is very probable she hath not dun much mischefe and if the honored counsel shall plese so grant me that favor I shall understand to leve her at punkapoag[.] . . . I shall obtaine so much favor from the honored counsel which will further oblige him who is your honored to command william hahaton

boston the 22: 7. 75 [September 22, 1675]

The 1675 petition of William Nahaton for the release of a relative sold into slavery.

Manitou and the City on a Hill

The Algonquian Indians in New England believed in many gods, or manitos [manitous], whom they worshiped through feasts, dances, and religious rituals. A Narragansett myth tells of the southwest god, Cautantowwit, who created man and woman and ruled an afterworld. The Wamapanoag Indians, neighbors to the Narragansetts, called Cautantowwit Kiehtan, and in 1624 told a curious English colonist about their beliefs.

At first, they say, there was no sachim or king, but Kiehtan, who dwelleth above in the heavens, whither all good men go when they die, to see their friends, and have their fill of all things. This his habitation lieth far westward in the heavens, they say; thither the bad men go also, and knock at his door, but he bids them quatchet, that is to say, walk abroad, for there is no place for such;

so that they wander in restless want and penury. Never man saw this Kiehtan; only old men tell them of him, and bid them tell their children, yea to charge them to teach their posterities the same, and lay the like charge upon them. This power they acknowledge to be good; and when they would obtain any great matter, meet together and cry unto him; and so likewise for plenty, victory, etc., sing, dance, feast, give thanks, and hang up garlands and other things in memory of the same.

During the first Puritans' voyage across the Atlantic aboard the *Arabella*, John Winthrop, governor of the Massachusetts Bay Colony, delivered an address to the men and women who would plant the colony. Winthrop reminded them of the colony's religious mission in founding a model Christian society, a "city on a hill" for all of Europe to see.

The only way to . . . provide for our posterity, is to followe the counsell of Micah, to do justly, to love mercy, to walk humbly with our God. For this end, wee must be knitt together, in this worke, as one man. Wee must entertaine each other in brotherly affection. Wee must be willing to abridge ourselves of our superfluities, merce [merge] together in all meekeness, gentlenes, patience and liberality. Wee must delight in eache other; make other's conditions our owne; rejoice together, mourne together, labour and suffer together, allwayes haueving before our eyes and our commission and community in the worke, as members of the same body. Soe shall wee keepe the unitie of the spirit in the bond of peace. The Lord will be our God, and delight to dwell among us, as his owne people, and will command a blessing upon us in all our wayes. Soe that wee shall see much more of his wisdome, power, goodness and truthe, than formerly wee have been acquainted with. Wee shall finde that the God of Israell is among us, when ten of us shall be able to resist a thousand of our enemies; when hee shall make us a prayse and glory that men shall say of succeeding plantations, "the Lord shall make it likely that of new England." For wee must consider that wee shall be as a citty upon a hill. The eies of all people are uppon us. Soe that if wee shall deale falsely with our God in this worke wee have undertaken, and soe cause him to withdrawe his present help from us, wee shall be made a story and a by-word through the world. Wee shall open the mouthes of enemies to speake evil of the wayes of God, and all professors for God's sake. Wee shall shame the faces of many of God's worthy servants, and cause theire prayers to be turned into curses upon us till wee be consumed out of the good land whither we are a goeing.

Roger Williams, who wrote *A Key into the Language of America*, in 1643 explained conversations he had had with the Narragansett Indians about religion. Williams was among the first Englishmen in New England to attempt to convert the Indians to Christianity, and his Key includes the text of many dialogues he had with the Narragansetts.

Manìt, manittówock.God, Gods.

Obs. [Observation] He that questions whether God made the World, the *Indians* will teach him. I must acknowledge I have received in my converse with them many Confirmations of those two great points, Heb. 11.6. viz:

1. That God is.

2. That hee is a rewarder of all them that diligently seek him.

They will generally confesse that God made all: but then in speciall, although they deny not that English-mans God made English Men, and the Heavens and Earth there! yet their Gods made them, and the Heaven and Earth where they dwell. . . .

First they branch their God-head into many Gods.

Secondly, attribute it to Creatures.

First, many Gods: they have given me the Names of thirty seven, which I have, all which in their soleme Worships they invocate as Kautántowwit the great South-West God, to whose House all soules goe, and from whom came their Corne, Beanes, as they say. . . . Even as the Papists have their He and Shee Saint Protectors as St. George, St. Patrick, St. Denis, Virgin Mary, etc. . . .

Secondly, as they have many of these fained Deities, so worship they the Creatures in whom they conceive doth rest some Deitie:

Keesuckquànd.	The Sun God.
Nanepaûshat.	The Moone God.
Paumpágussit.	The Sea God.
Yotáanit.	The Fire God.

Supposing that Deities be in these, &c.

When I have argued with them about their Fire-God: can it, say they, be but this fire must be a God, or Divine power, that out of a stone will arise in a Sparke, and when a poore naked Indian is ready to starve with cold in the House, and especially in the

On this page from Roger Williams's A Key into the Language of America, *he discusses the Narragansett Indians' ideas about religion.*

Of their Religion.   115

Obs. He that questions whether God made the World, the *Indians* will teach him. I must acknowledge I have received in my converse with them many Confirmations of those two great points, *Heb.* 11.6. *viz:*

1. That God is.

2. That hee is a rewarder of all them that diligently seek him.

They will generally confesse that God made all : but then in speciall although they deny not that *English-mans* God made *English* Men, and the Heavens and Earth there ! yet their Gods made them and the Heaven, and Earth where they dwell.

Nummusquauna- | *God is angry with me?*
muckqun manìt.

Obs. I have heard a poore *Indian* lamenting the losse of a child at break of day, call up his Wife and children, and all about him to Lamentation, and with abundance of teares cry out! O God thou hast taken away my child! thou art angry with me : O turne thine anger from me, and spare the rest of my children.

If they receive any good in hunting, fishing, Harvest &c. they acknowledge God in it.

Yea, if it be but an ordinary accident, a fall, &c. they will say God was angry and did it.

mus—

Woods, often saves his life, doth dresse all our Food for us, and if it be angry will burne the House about us, yea if a spark fall into the drie wood, burnes up the Country? (though this burning of the Wood to them they count a Benefit, both for destroying of vermin, and keeping downe the Weeds and thickets). . . .

Obs. After I had (as farre as my language would reach) discoursed (upon a time) before the chiefe Sachim or Prince of the Countrey, with his Archpriests, and many others in a full Assembly; and being night, wearied with travell and discourse, I lay down to rest; and before I slept, I heard this passage:

A Quinníhticut Indian (who had heard our discourse) told the Sachim Miantunnómu, that soules went not up to Heaven, or downe to Hell; For, saith he, Our fathers have told us, that our soules goe to the Southwest.

The Sachem answered, But how do you know your selfe, that your soules goe to the Southwest; did you ever see a soule goe thither?

The Native replyed; when did he (naming my selfe) see a soule goe to Heaven or Hell?

The Sachim againe replyed: He hath books and writings, and one which God himselfe made, concerning mens soules, and therefore may well know more than wee that have none, but take all upon trust from our forefathers.

Marking the Landscape

The Algonquian Indians in southern New England lived in small villages where the women planted crops of maize, beans, and squashes and the men hunted in the woods or fished along the waters. John Josselyn, an English visitor, described Algonquian settlements and remarked, as many colonists did, that the Indians' houses, or wigwams, were portable. At the change of seasons, whole villages might migrate to better terrain and hunting grounds. To Josselyn, the mobility of the Indian communities meant that they could not be considered towns in any strict sense. This belief developed in part as a rationalization to justify the colonists' seizure of Indian territory.

Their houses which they call *Wigwams*, are built with Poles pitcht into the ground of a round form for most part, sometimes square, they bind down the tops of their poles, leaving a hole for smoak to go out at, the rest they cover with the bark of Trees, and line the inside of their *Wigwams* with mats made of Rushes painted with several colours, one good post they set up in the middle that reaches to the hole in the top, with a staff a cross before it at a convenient height, they knock in a pin on which they hang their Kettle, beneath that they set up a broad stone for a back which keepeth the post from burning; round by the walls they spread their mats and skins where the men sleep whilst their women dress their victuals, they have commonly two doors, one opening to the South, the other to the North, and according as the wind sits, they close up one door with a bark and hang a *Dears* skin or the like before the other. Towns they have none, being always removing from one place to another for conveniency of food, sometimes to those places where one sort of fish is most plentiful, other whiles where others are. I have seen half a hundred of their *Wigwams* together in a piece of ground and they shew prettily, within a day or two, or a week they have been all dispersed.

The Algonquians believed that land could not be "owned" in the way Europeans understood ownership. They nonetheless made regular use of certain lands for hunting and planting, and controlled their environment in very deliberate ways: to enrich the soil and make hunting easier, they set forest fires, clearing out thick underbrush. English settlers, however, believed that the Indians had done nothing to "improve" the land, since they had not built permanent structures on it—fences, houses, barns, churches. It was this perception on the part of the English, that the land was "empty," that provided their justification for taking Indian territory. Robert Cushman, who journeyed to Plymouth on the *Mayflower* in 1620, explained why the English settlers could take Indian lands.

Their land is spacious and void, and they are few and do but run over the grass, as do also the foxes and wild beasts. They are not industrious, neither have they art, science, skill or faculty to use either the land or the commodities of it; but all spoils, rots, and is marred for want of manuring, gathering, ordering, etc. As the ancient patriarchs therefore removed from straighter places into more roomy ones, where the land lay idle and vasted and none used it, though there dwelt inhabitants by them (as in Gen. 13: 6, 11, 12, and 34: 21, and 41: 20), so is it lawful now to take a land which none useth and make use of it.

The Savages are accustomed to set fire of the Country in all places where they come, and to burne it twice a yeare, viz: at the Spring, and the fall of the leafe. The reason that mooves them to doe so, is because it would other wise be so overgrowne with underweedes that it would be all a coppice wood, and the people would not be able in any wise to passe through the Country out of a beaten path. . . .

And this custome of firing the Country is the meanes to make it passable; and by that meanes the trees growe here and there as in our parks: and makes the Country very beautifull and commodious.

—Thomas Morton, *New English Canaan* (1637)

In the summer of 1642, Miantonomi, a sachem or leader of the Narragansett Indians, addressed the neighboring Montauk Indians of Long Island with a plea for Indian unity. Miantonomi's speech reveals that the Algonquian Indians were deeply aware of the effects of English agriculture on native planting and hunting.

For so are we all Indians as the English are, and say brother to one another; so must we be one as they are, otherwise we shall all be gone shortly, for you know our fathers had plenty of deer and skins, our plains were full of deer, as also our woods, and of turkies, and our coves full of fish and fowl. But these English having gotten our land, they with scythes cut down the grass, and with axes fell the trees; their cows and horses eat the grass, and their hogs spoil our clam banks, and we shall all be starved.

Praying Indians

The Algonquians' religious beliefs were strongly held, but crises like the devastating epidemics during the first half of the 17th century led many to consider conversion to Christianity. During the early years of Puritan settlement, the colonists spent little energy fulfilling their mission to convert the native Algonquians. While the Indians and the colonists lived in close proximity and, as in Virginia, the colonists relied on the Indians' generosity to survive their first winters, few colonists bothered even to learn the Indians' language. In the 1640s, however, John Eliot began working with John Sassamon and several other Massachusett Indians to learn their language. With the help of his skilled Indian teachers and interpreters, Eliot began preaching to small groups of Indians and soon set up villages known as praying towns, where newly converted Christian Indians could live and worship. For a New England Indian, becoming Christian meant abandoning much of his traditional culture. Here, Eliot recounts a meeting with a group of Indians considering conversion to Christianity in 1647. Eliot lists first the Indians' questions, followed by his own responses.

How may we come to know Jesus Christ?

Our first answer was, that if they were able to read our Bible, the book of God, therein they should see most clearly what Jesus Christ was: but because they could not do that; therefore,

Secondly, we wished them to think, and meditate of so much as had been taught them, and which they now heard of our Gods book, and to think much and often upon it, both when they did lie down on their mats in their wigwams, and when they rose up, and to go alone in the fields and woods, and muse on it, and so God would teach them, especially if they used a third help, which was,

Prayer to God to teach them and reveal Jesus Christ unto them; and we tole them that although they could not make any long prayers as the English could, yet if they did but sigh and groan, and say thus; Lord make me know Jesus Christ for I know him not, and if they did say so again and again with their hearts that God would teach them Jesus Christ, because he is such a God as will be found of them that seek him with all their hearts, and he is a God hearing the prayers of all men both Indian as well as English, and that English men by this means have come to the knowledge of Jesus Christ. . . .

These things were spoken by him who had preached to them in their own language, borrowing now and then some small help from the interpreter whom we brought with us, and who could oftentimes express our minds more distinctly than any of us could; but this we perceived, that a few words from the preacher were more regarded than many from the Indian interpreter.

One of them after this answer, replied to us, that he was a little while since praying in his wigwam, unto God and Jesus Christ, that God would give him a good heart, and that while he was praying, one of his fellow Indians interrupted him, and told him, that he prayed in vain, because Jesus Christ understood not what Indians speak in prayer, he had been used to hear English men pray and so could well enough understand them, but Indian language in prayer he thought he was not acquainted with it, but was a stranger to it, and therefore could not understand them. His question therefore was, whether Jesus Christ did understand, or God did understand Indian prayers.

This question sounding just like themselves, we studied to give as familiar an answer as we could, and therefore in this as in all other our answers, we endeavored to speak nothing without clearing of it up by some familiar similitude; our answer summarily was therefore this, that Jesus Christ and God by him made all things, and makes all men, not only English but Indian men, and if he had made them both (which we know the light of nature would readily teach as they had been also instructed by us) then he knew all that was within man and came from man, all his desires, and all his

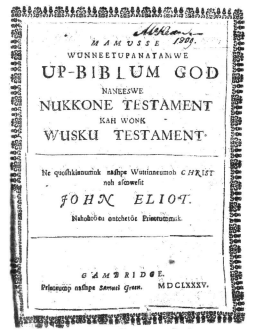

John Eliot's translation of the Bible into the language of the Algonquians appeared in 1663. It was the first Bible printed in America.

thoughts, and all his speeches, and so all his prayer, and if he made Indian men, then he knows all Indian prayers also: and therefore we bid them look upon that Indian basket that was before them, there was black and white straws, and many other things they made it of, now though others did not know what those things were who made not the basket, yet he that made it must needs tell all the things in it, so (we said) it was here.

In order to become Christians, Indians in New England, like all Puritans, were required to undergo a formal conversion in which they confessed their sins before the elders of the church. Totherswamp, an early convert, read the following confession aloud to a group of Puritan elders and explained the difficulties of his conversion. Like many "praying Indians," Totherswamp had been deeply skeptical of the Puritans' religion and considered converting only after many of his family and friends had died from European-induced diseases, leaving him to find a new community.

Before I prayed unto god, the English, when I came unto their houses, often said to me, Pray to God; but I having many friends who loved me, and I loved them, and they cared not for praying to God, and therefore I did not: But I thought in my heart, that if my friends should die, and I live, I then would pray to God; soon after, God so wrought that they did almost all die, few of them left; and then my heart feared, and I thought, that now I will pray unto God, and yet I was ashamed to pray; and if I eat and did not pray, I was ashamed of that also; so that I had a double shame upon me: Then you came unto us, and taught us, and said unto us, *Pray unto God;* and after that, my heart grew strong, and I was no more ashamed to pray, but I did take up praying to God; yet at first I did not think of God and eternal Life, but only that the English should love me and I loved them: But after I came to learn what sin was, by the Commandements of God, and then I saw all my sins, lust, gaming, &c . . . You taught, That Christ knoweth all our hearts, and seeth what is in them, if humility, or anger, or evil thoughts, Christ seeth all that is in the heart; then my heart feared greatly, because God was angry for all my sins; yea, now my heart is full of evil thoughts, and my heart runs away from God, therefore my heart feareth and mourneth. Every day I see sin in my heart; one man brought sin into the World, and I am full of that sin, and I break Gods Word every day. I see I deserve not pardon, for the first mans sinnins; I can do no good, for I am like the Devil, nothing but evil thoughts, and words, and works. . . . but Christ hath done for us all righteousness, and died for us because of our sins, and Christ teacheth us, That if we cast away our sins, and trust in Christ, then God will pardon all our sins; this I beleeve Christ hath done, I can do no righteousness, but Christ hath done it for me; this I beleeve, and therefore I do hope for pardon. When I first heard the Commandements, I then took up praying to God and cast off sin. Again, When I heard, and understood my Redemption by Christ, then I beleeved Jesus Christ to take away my sins: every Commandement taught me sin,

John Eliot was called the "Apostle to the Indians." His determination to Christianize the Indians led him to establish villages for the converted. He and his helpers founded 14 such communities on lands granted for that purpose by colonial authorities. The "praying Indians," however, were caught between hostile tribes and Indian-hating whites during King Philip's War and most were killed. White settlements took over many of the villages that Eliot had established.

and my duty to God. When you ask me why do I love God? I answer, Because he giveth me all outward blessings, as food, clothing, children, all gifts of strength, speech, hearing; especially that he giveth us a Minister to teach us, and giveth us Government; and my heart feareth lest Government should reprove me; but the greatest mercy of all is Christ, to give us pardon and life.

As part of John Eliot's missionary efforts, he and several Indian interpreters translated the entire King James Bible into the Massachusett language. A printing press was shipped from England for the special purpose of printing the Bible and other texts in what would come to be called the Indian library.

Christian Indians who owned Bibles often used the margins of the pages to practice their writing skills. The owner of one Bible wrote:

I Nannahdinnoo, this is my book, and I tanoukqussa this. I tanookqussa it. I, I Nanahdinnoo, own this forever. Because I bought it with my money and not with assookuhkatchagmoon.

Timeline

1273–95
Marco Polo voyages to China

c.1400–1600
Iroquois confederate into Peoples of the Longhouse

1405–33
Voyages of Cheng Ho, Chinese explorer

1406
Claudius Ptolemy's writings translated into Latin

c.1450
Export of African slaves to continental Europe and sugar plantations on the Atlantic islands begins

Gutenberg invents the printing press

1472
Isidore's T-O map becomes the first map printed in Europe

1477
Marco Polo's *Travels* published

1487
Bartolomeu Dias, Portuguese explorer, sails around the southern tip of Africa

1492
Columbus's first voyage

1493
Pope Alexander VI issues papal bull, dividing the new-found lands between Spain and Portugal

1493–94
Columbus's second voyage (Lesser Antilles, Virgin Islands, Puerto Rico, and the south coast of Cuba and Jamaica)

1497
John Cabot sails to Newfoundland (possibly the first landfall on mainland)

1498
John Cabot departs on his second voyage and is never heard from again

Spanish colony begins on Hispaniola

1498–1500
Columbus's third voyage (the mainland)

1498
Vasco de Gama extends Dias's route all the way to India

1501–?
Amerigo Vespucci sails to the coast of Brazil

c.1502
Malinalli, later called "La Malinche," born

1502–1504
Columbus's final voyage

1503
Vespucci's *Mundus Novus* first published

1507
Waldseemüller's world map uses "America"

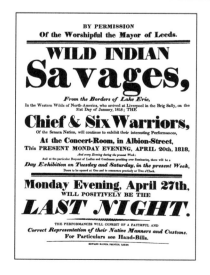

1513

Juan Ponce de Leon sights and names Florida, which he believes to be an island

1513

Vasco Núñez de Balboa makes a land crossing over Panama to the Pacific

1514

Spanish *requerimiento* put into effect

1519–22

Magellan circumnavigates the globe

1519-21

Cortés explores Mexico

1519

La Malinche and 19 other Indian women are presented as a gift to Cortés during his march through Tabasco

1524

Giovanni da Verrazano commissioned by Francis I, King of France, to sail to the New World

1527

Las Casas's *Historia de las Indias* published

1528

Panfilo de Navaez (Spanish) arrives by ship on the western coast of Florida; later his ships are lost at sea and Alvar Nuñez de Vaca is shipwrecked on an island off the coast of Texas

1534

Jacques Cartier makes the first of three voyages—first to Newfoundland, then into the interior of Canada

1535

Cartier's second voyage

1539

De Soto expedition

c.1540

La Malinche dies

1540–42

Francisco Vasquez de Coronado marches to interior of California, to Zuni pueblos, and into New Mexico and Kansas

1542

Juan Rodriguez Cabrillo explores the coast of Alta California; arrives at San Diego, Santa Monica, and parts northward

1550

Debate at Valladolid between Las Casas and Sepúlveda

1558

Hernando de Soto (Spain) leads expedition to Florida and into the interior, by land—finds Mississippi River

1569

Mercator Map created

1577–80

Sir Francis Drake circumnavigates the globe

1583

Sir Humphrey Gilbert sails to Newfoundland

1584

Raleigh reconnoiters Virginia and kidnaps Manteo and Wanchese; Hakluyt's "Discourse on Western Planting"

1585

Sir Richard Grenville leads fleet and English colonize Roanoke Island, but they leave in 1586; John White paints the Virginia Algonquians

1586–88

Cavendish circumnavigates the globe

1587

A second colony is planted at Roanoke, but abandoned, its fate unknown

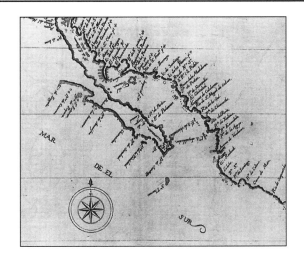

1588
Spanish Armada's attempt to invade England fails

1595
Pocahontas is born

c.1600
Powhatan Indians unite under Powhatan

1602
Dutch East India Company chartered

1606
Creation of the Virginia Company

1607
Jamestown founded

John Smith is taken captive by Powhatan and adopted into the Algonquian community

1608
Champlain founds Quebec

1609
English establish a colony in Bermuda

Henry Hudson explores and names Hudson Bay and River

1611
Pieter van den Keere's double-hemisphere map of the world

1612
Captain Samuel Argall takes Pocahontas captive

1614
Pocahontas marries John Rolfe

1616
Pocahontas travels to England and is received at court

1617
Pocahontas dies

1619
First Africans brought to the English North American mainland

1620
Pilgrims arrive in Plymouth

1621
Dutch West India Company chartered

1623
English and French settle St. Christopher

1624
Treaty of trade between Iroquois and New France

1625
English occupy Barbados

1631
Governor John Winthrop arrives in New England

1635
The French colonize Guadeloupe and Martinique

1639
Marie de l'Incarnation sails to Quebec and establishes the Ursuline convent

1643
Iroquois sign treaty with the French

1650
By this date, Africans constitute the majority of migrants to the Americas

1653
Montreal Treaty between French and Iroquois

1657
Bressani creates map of New France

1663
"Indian Bible" published in Cambridge

1664
New Netherlands becomes English

1675–76
King Philip's War

1676
Kateri Tekakwitha is baptized at Kahnawake

1699
Maria Sibylla Merian and her daughter sail to Suriname

1745
Olaudah Equiano born in Nigeria

1769
Junípero Serra founds mission in San Diego

1789
Equiano's autobiography published

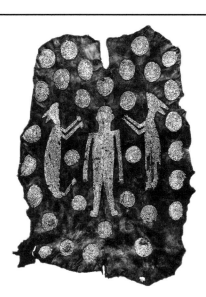

Further Reading

Axtell, James. *After Columbus: Essays in the Ethnohistory of Colonial North America.* New York: Oxford University Press, 1988.

———. *Beyond 1492: Encounters in Colonial North America.* New York: Oxford University Press, 1992.

Bagrow, Leo. *History of Cartography.* Chicago: Precedent Publishing,1985.

Bradford, William. *History of Plymouth Plantation, 1620–1647.* Samuel Eliot Morison, ed. New York: Knopf, 1952.

Berlin, Ira. *Many Thousands Gone: The First Two Centuries of Slavery in North America.* Cambridge: Cambridge University Press, 1998.

Cabeza de Vaca, Alvar Nuñez Diaz. *Castaways: The Narrative of Alvar Nuñez Cabeza de Vaca.* Enrique Pupo-Walker, ed. Berkeley: University of California Press, 1993.

Calloway, Colin. *New Worlds for All: Indians, Europeans, and the Remaking of Early America.* Baltimore: Johns Hopkins University Press, 1997.

Columbus, Christopher. *Journals and Other Documents.* Samuel Eliot Morison, trans. New York: Heritage, 1963.

Cortés, Hernan. *Five Letters, 1519–1526.* New York: Norton, 1993.

Cronon, William. *Changes in the Land: Indians, Colonists, and the Ecology of New England.* New York: Hill and Wang, 1983.

Crosby, Alfred. *The Columbian Exchange: Biological and Cultural Consequences of 1492.* Westport, Conn.: Greenwood Press, 1973.

———. *Ecological Imperialism: The Biological Expansion of Europe, 900–1900.* London: Cambridge University Press, 1986.

Davidson, James West, and Mark Hamilton Lytle. *After the Fact: The Art of Historical Detection.* New York: Knopf, 1982.

Davis, Natalie Zemon. *Women on the Margins: Three Seventeenth-Century Lives.* Cambridge and London: Cambridge University Press, 1995.

Demos, John. *The Tried and the True: Native American Women Confronting Colonization.* New York: Oxford University Press, 1995.

———. *The Unredeemed Captive: A Family Story from Early America.* New York: Knopf, 1995.

Diaz, Bernal. *The Conquest of New Spain.* New York: Penguin, 1963.

Dor-Ner, Zvi. *Columbus and the Age of Discovery.* New York: Morrow, 1991.

DuBois, Ellen Carol, and Vicki L. Ruiz, eds. *Unequal Sisters: A Multi-Cultural Reader in U.S. Women's History.* 2nd ed. New York: Routledge, 1994.

Dunn, Oliver, and James E. Kelley, eds. *Diario of Christopher Columbus' First Voyage to America, 1492–1493.* Norman: University of Oklahoma Press, 1989.

Elliott, J.H. *The Old World and the New, 1492–1650.* Cambridge: Cambridge University Press, 1970.

Equiano, Olaudah. *The Interesting Narrative of the Life of Olaudah Equiano.* Paul Edwards, ed. New York: Praeger, 1967.

Gates, Jr., Henry Louis, ed. *Classic Slave Narratives.* New York: Penguin, 1987.

Goss, John. *The Mapmaker's Art: An Illustrated History of Cartography.* Skokie, Ill.: Rand McNally, 1993.

Gunn, Giles, ed. *Early American Writing.* New York: Penguin, 1994.

Jennings, Francis. *The Founders of America.* New York: Norton, 1993.

Jordan, Winthrop D. *White over Black: American Attitudes toward the Negro, 1550–1812.* New York: Norton, 1977.

Josephy, Jr., Alvin M., ed. *America in 1492: The World of the Indian Peoples before the Arrival of Columbus.* New York: Knopf, 1992.

Kolchin, Peter. *American Slavery, 1619–1877.* New York: Hill and Wang, 1993.

Las Casas, Bartolomé de. *In Defense of the Indians.* Translated and edited by Stafford Poole. Dekalb: Northern Illinois University Press, 1992.

Leon-Portilla, Miguel, ed. *The Broken Spears: The Aztec Account of the Conquest of Mexico.* Boston: Beacon Press, 1962.

Lepore, Jill. *The Name of War: King Philip's War and the Origins of American Identity.* New York: Knopf, 1998.

Lunenfeld, Marvin. *1492: Discovery, Invasion, Encounter.* Lexington, Mass.: D.C. Heath, 1991.

Mancall, Peter C., and James H. Merrell, eds. *American Encounters: Natives and Newcomers from European Contact to Indian Removal, 1500–1850.* New York: Routledge, 2000.

Morgan, Edmund. *American Slavery, American Freedom: The Ordeal of Colonial Virginia.* New York: Norton, 1975.

Morison, Samuel Eliot. *The European Discovery of America: The Southern Voyages, A.D. 1492–1616.* New York: Oxford University Press, 1974.

Moynihan, Ruth Barnes, et al. *Second to None: A Documentary History of American Women.* Lincoln: University of Nebraska Press, 1993.

Mullin, Michael, ed. *American Negro Slavery: A Documentary History.* Columbia: University of South Carolina Press, 1976.

Nash, Gary. *Red, White, and Black: The Peoples of Early America.* Englewood Cliffs, N.J.: Prentice Hall, 1974.

Palmer, Colin A. *The First Passage: Blacks in the Americas, 1502–1617.* New York: Oxford University Press, 1995.

Parry, J.H. *The Age of Reconnaissance.* Berkeley: University of California Press, 1981.

Quinn, David, ed. *New American World: A Documentary History of North America to 1612.* 5 vols. New York: Arno Press, 1979.

Richter, Daniel K. *The Ordeal of the Longhouse: The Peoples of the Iroquois League in the Era of European Colonization.* Chapel Hill: University of North Carolina Press, 1992.

Schwartz, Seymour I., and Ralph E. Ehrenberg. *The Mapping of America.* New York: Abrams, 1980.

Shoemaker, Nancy. *Negotiators of Change: Historical Perspectives on Native American Women.* New York: Routledge, 1995.

Stannard, David E. *American Holocaust: The Conquest of the New World.* New York: Oxford University Press, 1992.

Smith, John. *Captain John Smith: A Select Edition of His Writings.* Karen Kupperman, ed. Chapel Hill: University of North Carolina Press, 1988.

Stefoff, Rebecca. *Accidental Explorers: Surprises and Side Trips in the History of Discovery.* New York: Oxford University Press, 1992.

———. *The Young Oxford Companion to Maps and Mapmaking.* New York: Oxford University Press, 1995.

Sturtevant, Ed. *Handbook of the North American Indians.* 15 vols. Washington, D.C.: Smithsonian Institution, 1990.

Weber, David J. *The Spanish Frontier in North America.* New Haven: Yale University Press, 1992.

Whitfield, Peter. *The Image of the World: Twenty Centuries of World Maps.* San Francisco: Pomegranate, 1994.

Wolff, Hans, ed. *America: Early Maps of the New World.* Munich: Prestel, 1992.

Wood, Dennis. *The Power of Maps.* New York: Guilford, 1992.

Wood, Peter H. *Strange New Land: African Americans, 1617–1776.* New York: Oxford University Press, 1995.

Wright, Donald R. *African Americans in the Colonial Era: From African Origins through the American Revolution.* Arlington Heights, Ill.: Harlan Davidson, 1990.

Text Credits

Main Text

p. 35-36: From *Broken Spears* by Miguel Leon-Portilla, 4-6. © 1962, 1990 by Miguel Leon-Portilla. Expanded and Updated Edition © 1992 by Miguel Leon-Portilla. Reprinted by permission of Beacon Press, Boston.

p. 36-37: Silas T. Rand, *Legends of the Micmacs* (New York: Longmans, Green, and Co., 1894), 225-226.

p. 37-38: David Quinn, ed., *New American World: A Documentary History of North America to 1612*, (New York: Arno Press, 1979), I: 84.

p. 38-39: F.G. Davenport, ed., *European Treaties Bearing on the History of the United States and Its Dependencies to 1648* (Washington, D.C., 1917), I: 75-78.

p. 40-42: Excerpt from *Diario of Christopher Columbus's First Voyage to America, 1492-1493*. Transcribed and translated by Oliver C. Dunn and James E. Kelley, Jr. (Norman, Oklahoma: University of Oklahoma Press, 1989), 65-73.

p. 43: F.A. MacNutt, trans. *De Orbe Novo: The Eight Decades of Peter Martyr D'Anghera* (New York: G.P. Putnam's Sons, 1912), 176.

p. 43-44: Olaudah Equiano, *The Interesting Narrative of the Life of Olaudah Equiano or Gustavus Vassa, the African, Written by Himself* (London, 1789).

p. 44: Bernal Díaz del Castillo, *The Discovery and Conquest of Mexico, 1517-1521*, ed. Irving A. Leonard (New York: Farrar, Straus & Giroux, Inc., 1966), 61-62.

p. 45-46: Ramsay Cook, *The Voyages of Jacques Cartier* (Toronto: University of Toronto Press, 1993), 111. Used by permission of the publisher.

p. 46: Roger Williams, *A Key into the Language of America* (London, 1643), 111.

p. 47-48: Américo Vespucio, *El Nuevo Mundo*, Roberto Levillier, ed. (Buenos Aires, Editorial Nova, 1951), 276; 290-92.

p. 48-49: *Native American Testimony* by Peter Nabokov, 58. Copyright © 1978, 1979, 1991 by Peter Nabokov; Foreword Copyright © 1991 by Vine Deloria, Jr. Used by permission of Viking Penguin, a division of Penguin Putnam Inc.

p. 50: William Wood, *New England's Prospect* (Boston: Prince Society, 1865), I: 105-110.

p. 51, top: James Axtell, ed., *The Indian Peoples of Eastern America: A Documentary History of the Sexes* (New York: Oxford University Press, 1981), 106-7.

p. 51, bottom: Axtell, *The Indian Peoples*, 102.

p. 52-53: Fisher, Dexter, ed. *The Third Woman: Minority Women Writers of the United States*, 44. Copyright © 1980 by Houghton Mifflin Company. Used with permission.

p. 53: Genesis 2:21-24; 3:16. King James Bible.

p. 55-56: Quinn, *New American World*, I: 283.

p. 56: Quinn, *New American World*, I: 157.

p. 57: From *Native American Testimony* by Peter Nabokov, 26. Copyright © 1978, 1979, 1991 by Peter Nabokov; Foreword Copyright © 1991 by Vine Deloria, Jr. Used by permission of Viking Penguin, a division of Penguin Putnam Inc.

p. 62: From *Broken Spears* by Miguel Leon-Portilla © 1962, 1990 by Miguel Leon-Portilla, 25-26; 29. Expanded and Updated Edition © 1992 by Miguel Leon-Portilla. Reprinted by permission of Beacon Press, Boston.

p. 63-65: From *Broken Spears* by Miguel Leon-Portilla © 1962, 1990 by Miguel Leon-Portilla, 63-65. Expanded and Updated Edition © 1992 by Miguel Leon-Portilla. Reprinted by permission of Beacon Press, Boston.

p. 65-67: Anthony Pagden, ed., *Hernán Cortés, Letters from Mexico* (New Haven: Yale University Press, 1986), 84-86.

p. 67-68: From *Broken Spears* by Miguel Leon-Portilla, 92-93. © 1962, 1990 by Miguel Leon-Portilla. Expanded and Updated Edition © 1992 by Miguel Leon-Portilla. Reprinted by permission of Beacon Press, Boston.

p. 68-70: de Vaca, A. Nuñéz Cabeza. *Castaways: The Narrative of Alvar Nunez Cabeza de Vaca*, translated/edited by Walker, Enrique Pupo, pp. 49-50, 71-72. Reference #DOC 3-7, 3-16. Copyright © 1993 The Regents of the University of California.

p. 71-72: Quinn, *New American World*, I: 425-428.

p. 73-74: Arthur Helps, *The Spanish Conquest in America* (London, 1855), I: 264-267.

p. 74-75: Quinn, *New American World*, II: 160-161; 168.

p. 76-77: Bartolomé de Las Casas, *In Defense of the Indians*, translated and edited by Stafford Poole (DeKalb: Northern Illinois University Press, 1992), 25-27. Courtesy of Northern Illinois University Press.

p. 77-78: Excerpts from "Sepulveda" in *Latin American History: Select Problems, Identity, Integration and Nationhood* by Frederick B. Pike, 47-52. Copyright © 1969 by Harcourt, Inc., reprinted by permission of the publisher.

p. 80-83: Junipero Serra, *Writings*, ed. Antoine Tibesar (Washington, D.C., 1955-1966), I: 191, 209, 225-227, 257, 267; II: 79, 87-89. Academy of American Franciscan History.

p. 83-85: Minna and Gordon Hewes, "Indian Life and Customs at Mission San Luis Rey: A Record of California Mission Life, Written by Pablo Tac, an Indian Neophyte," *The Americas* 9 (10), July 1952, 93-99.

p. 88-89: Iroquois confederacy. In Giles Gunn, *Early American Writing* (New York: Penguin, 1994), 16-19.

p. 89-90: Calvin Martin, *Keepers of the Game: Indian-Animal Relationships and the Fur Trade* (Berkeley: University of California Press, 1978), 107.

p. 92-93: Cook, *Voyages of Jacques Cartier*, 24-27.

p. 94-95: W.L. Grant, ed., *Voyages of Samuel de Champlain, 1604-1618* (New York: Barnes & Noble, Inc., 1907), 150-152.

p. 95-96: William F. Ganong, trans. and ed., *New Relation of Gaspesia, with the Customs and Religion of the Gaspesian Indians*, by Christien LeClerq (Toronto: Champlain Society, 1910), 104-106.

p. 96-98: François de Crepieul, "The Life of a Montagnaix Missionary, presented to his Successors in the Montagnaix Mission for their Instruction and Greater Consolation," 1697. *Jesuits: Letters from Missions (North America). The Jesuit Relations and Allied Documents* (Cleveland: Burrows Bros. Co., 1896-1901), 64: 43-49.

p. 99-100: *Jesuits: Letters from Missions (North America). The Jesuit Relations and Allied Documents* (Cleveland: Burrows Bros. Co., 1896-1901), 24: 295-297.

p. 104-105: Jennings, Francis, ed., *The History and Culture of Iroquois Diplomacy*. Syracuse: Syracuse University Press, 1985. pp. 137-139. Used by permission of the publisher.

p. 109-112: Quinn, *New American World*, III: 118-121.

p. 112-113: Ralph Lane, letter to Richard Hakluyt the Elder, Sept. 3, 1585, reprinted in David B. Quinn and Alison M. Quinn, eds., *Virginia Voyages from Hakluyt* (London: Oxford University Press, 1973), 22-23.

p. 113-114: Quinn and Quinn, eds., *Virginia Voyages from Hakluyt*, 101-102.

p. 114-115: Thomas Hariot, *A Briefe Relation and True Report of the New Found Land of Virginia*, 1588, reprinted in Quinn and Quinn, eds., *Virginia Voyages from Hakluyt*, 48-49.

p. 116: From *Captain John Smith: A Selected Edition of His Writings*, edited by Karen Ordahl Kupperman, 174-175. Copyright © 1988 by the University of North Carolina Press. Used by permission of the publisher.

p. 117-119: From *Captain John Smith: A Selected Edition of His Writings*, edited by Karen Ordahl Kupperman, 111-114. Copyright © 1988 by the University of North Carolina Press. Used by permission of the publisher.

p. 120-121: Francis Bacon, "Of Plantations," (1625). From Samuel Harvey Reynolds, ed., *The Essays, or Counsels, Civil and Moral of Francis Bacon* (1890), 237-240.

p. 122-123: Lyon G. Tyler, ed., *Narratives of Early Virginia* (New York, 1907), 239-244.

p. 130-132: Olaudah Equiano, *Interesting Narrative*. Halifax edition, 1814.

p. 132-133: Jeffries MSS., XIV.3, Bristol Public Library, Bristol, England. Reprinted in Elizabeth Donnan, *Documents Illustrative of the History of the Slave Trade to America* (Washington D.C.: Carnegie Institution of Washington, 1930-1935), II: 327-328. Used by permission of the publisher.

p. 134-135: Donnan, *Documents*, I: 209, 226-234. Used by permission of the publisher.

p. 136: Olaudah Equiano, *Interesting Narrative*. Halifax edition, 1814. 63-65.

p. 137 (top): Donnan, *Documents*, I: 206. Used by permission of the publisher.

p. 137-138: Mary Prince, *The History of Mary Prince, a West Indian Slave, Related by Herself* (London, 1831). Reprinted in William L. Andrews, ed., *Six Women's Slave Narratives* (New York: Oxford University Press, 1988).

p. 139-140: Hugh Jones, *The Present State of Virginia*, ed. Richard L. Morton (1724).

p. 141-142: Prince, *The History of Mary Prince*.

p. 143: "The African Slave Trade Defended: And Corruption the Worst of Slaveries," *London Magazine* IX (1740): 493-494.

p. 143-144: Prince, *The History of Mary Prince*.

p. 145: Michael Mullin, ed., *American Negro Slavery: A Documentary History* (Columbia, South Carolina: University of South Carolina Press, 1976), 83.

p. 150: John Easton, "A Relacion of the Indyan War" (1675), reprinted in Charles H. Lincoln, ed., *Narratives of the Indian Wars, 1675-1699* (New York: Charles Scribner's Sons, 1913), 10-11.

p. 151-152: Mary Rowlandson, *The Sovereignty and Goodness of God* (1682; reprint, Boston: Bedford, 1992), 86.

p. 153-154: Massachusetts State Archives. Mass. Archives; Series 45X. Volume 30: #173. *John Elliot to the Massachusetts Council.* Dated 13 August 1675.

p. 155: Massachusetts State Archives. Mass. Archives; Series 45X. Volume 30: #176. *Petition by William Nahatan to the Massachusetts Council.* Dated 22 September 1676.

p. 156-157: John Winthrop, "A Modell of Christian Charity," 1630; *MHSC* 3rd ser., 7 (1838): 33-34, 44-48. Courtesy Massachusetts Historical Society.

p. 157-158: Williams, *Key Into the Language*, 109-117.

p. 158-159: John Josselyn, *An Account of Two Voyages to New England* (London, 1674), 126-127.

p. 162-163: Totherswamp's speech in John Eliot and Thomas Mayhew, *Tears of Repentence, Or, A Further Narrative of the Progress of the Gospell among the Indians in New-England* (London, 1653), 229-230.

Sidebars

p. 12: Sadekanaktie, 1694. Colin G. Calloway, ed. *The World Turned Upside Down: Indian Voices from Early America* (Boston: Bedford, 1994), 20.

p. 13: Lazzaro Buonamico, 1539, in J. H. Elliot, *The Old World and the New, 1492-1650* (Cambridge: Cambridge University Press, 1970), 72.

p. 15: Elliot, *Old World and the New*, 78.

p. 16: Axtell, *Beyond 1492*, 138.

p. 17: Elliot, *Old World and New*, 33.

p. 34: Michel de Montaigne, *Essays* (1580; reprint, New York: Viking, 1993).

p. 44: A. M. Stevens-Arroyo, *Cave of the Jaguar: The Mythological World of the Taínos* (Albuquerque: University of New Mexico Press, 1988), 88-176.

p. 45: Bernal Díaz del Castillo, *The Discovery and Conquest of Mexico, 1517-1521* (1522; reprint, New York: Da Capo, 1996), 59.

p. 49: Juan de Batanzos, *Cronicas Peruanas de Interes Indigena*, ed. F. Esteve Barba (Biblioteca de Autores Espanolas, vol. 209, Madrid, 1968), 7.

p. 60: Díaz, *The Discovery and Conquest of Mexico*, 72-73.

p. 70: Quinn, *New American World*, I: 428.

p. 74: Quinn, *New American World*, I: 160-161.

p. 75: Quinn, *New American World*, I: 168.

p. 90: Champlain, *Voyages*, 289.

p. 90: Samuel de Champlain, in *Jesuit Relations*, 5: 211; 10:26.

}{p. 92: Cook, *Voyages of Jacques Cartier*, 61.

p. 96: Colin G. Calloway, *New Worlds for All: Indians, Europeans, and the Remaking of Early America* (Baltimore, Md.: Johns Hopkins University Press, 1997), 43.

p. 97: *Jesuit Relations*, vol. 43, 156-185.

p. 98: Marie de l'Incarnation, *Correspondence*, ed. Dom Guy Oury (Solesmes: Abbaye Saint-Pierre, 1971), no. 50, 117-18; translated and reprinted in Natalie Zemon Davis, *Women on the Margins: Three Seventeenth-Century Lives* (New York: Cambridge University Press, 1995), 111-12.

p. 101: Marie de L'Incarnation, *Correspondence*, no. 50, 121.

p. 117: Hulme, *Colonial Encounters*, 144.

p. 122: Hulme, *Colonial Encounters*, 146.

p. 123: Hulme, *Colonial Encounters*, 146.

p. 131: Ottobah Cugoana, *Thoughts and Sentiments of the Evil and Wicked Traffic of the Slavery and Commerce of the Human Species*, 1787; reprinted in Francis D. Adams and Barry Sanders, eds., *Three Black Writers in Eighteenth-Century England* (Belmont, Calif.: Wadsworth, 1971), 52.

p. 134: Bernard Martin and Mark Spurrell, eds., *The Journals of a Slave Trader (John Newton), 1750-1754* (London: Epworth Press, 1962), 32.

p. 139: Davis, *Women on the Margins*, 185-86.

p. 140: Peter Kolchin and Eric Foner, eds. *American Slavery: 1619-1877* (New York: Hill and Wang, 1992), 11.

p. 145: Willie Lee Rose, ed., *A Documentary History of Slavery in North America* (New York: Oxford University Press, 1976), 20.

p. 148: Thomas Morton, *New English Canaan* (1637; reprint, New York: Burt Franklin, 1967), 132-33.

p. 159: Morton, *New English Canaan*, 172-73.

Picture Credits

Abby Aldrich Rockefeller Folk Art Center, Williamsburg, Va.: 142; American Museum of Natural History: 60, 66 (Neg. 326597), 67 (Neg. 120227); Ashmolean Museum, Oxford: 115; Bancroft Library Picture Collection: 80, 81, 85; Biblioteca Medicea Laurenziana, Florence: 24-25, 35; Biblioteca Nacional, Madrid, Spain: 62; Bibliothèque Nationale de France, Paris: 14, 15, 86-87; Bildarchiv Preussischer Kultur Besitz, Berlin: 41; by permission of the British Library: 7, 17, 20, 21, 22-23, 63, 73, 76, 93, 106, 113, 130 (top & bottom), 136; British Museum: 9, 23, 43 (Museum of Mankind), 54 (all), 108; British Public Record Office: 30; John Carter Brown Library: 9, 99; Colonial Williamsburg Foundation: 28-29; Thomas Fisher Rare Book Library, University of Toronto: 100; Werner Forman/Art Resource, NY: 127; Giraudon/Art Resource, NY: 46; Courtesy of The Hispanic Society of America, New York: 77; by permission of the

Houghton Library, Harvard University: 79; Library of Congress: frontispiece, 10, 23 (Duke of Alba's Collection), 32, 40, 42, 55, 58, 78, 95 (Rare Book Room), 108, 121, 138 (both), 161, 163; The Library of Virginia: 140; Courtesy of Massachusetts Archives: 148, 155; Massachusetts Historical Society, Boston: 149, 151; National Gallery of Canada, Ottawa: 101; National Library of Canada: 24, 90; National Museums and Galleries on Merseyside, Liverpool Museum: 29; Newberry Library: 13, 21, 31, 89, 116, 157; Collection of the New-York Historical Society: title page; New York Public Library: 48 (Print Collection, Miriam and Ira D. Wallach Division of Art, Prints and Photographs, Astor, Lenox, and Tilden Foundations), 50, 68 (Rare Book Room), 102, 124 (Picture Collection, The Branch Libraries), 146 (Rare Book Room), 152 (Rare Book Room); Courtesy of the Osher Map Library and Smith Center for Carto-

graphic Education, University of Southern Maine: 111; Photofest © The Walt Disney Company. All Rights Reserved: 123; The Pierpont Morgan Library, New York: 133 (MA 3900, f.100); Schloss Wolfegg, Würtemberg: 18-19; Schomburg Center for Research in Black Culture, New York Public Library: 129; Alexis Siroc: 12, 82, 126, 128; Smithsonian Institution, National Anthropological Archives: 71 (Photo No. 2267-E); Collection of the Supreme Court of the United States: 6; Taylor Museum of the Colorado Springs Fine Arts Center: 80; Tozzer Library, Harvard University: 92; Trinity College, Oxford: 114; Virginia State Library and Archives: 122; The William and Mary Quarterly (48:1, Jan. 1991): 119; Western History Collections, University of Oklahoma Library: 58 bottom; the Western Reserve Historical Society: 72, 77.

Index

About the Author

Jill Lepore is an associate professor of history and American studies at Boston University. She has been a fellow at the Charles Warren Center, Harvard University; the Bunting Institute, Radcliffe College; and the Humanities Foundation, Boston University. She is the author of *The Name of War: King Philip's War and the Origins of American Identity* (1998), winner of the Bancroft Prize, the Ralph Waldo Emerson Award, and the Berkshire Prize; and *A Is for American: Letters and Other Characters in the Newly United States* (2002). She is cofounder and coeditor of the web history magazine Common-place (www.common-place.org).